A Tale of Two SOULS
My Hand of GOD Story

ILANA DANNEMAN

Illustrated by:
Debra Sifen

Copyright© 2014 Ilana Danneman
All rights reserved.
ISBN #978-0-9860749-1-2
10 9 8 7 6 5 4 3

"Where you go I will go, and where you stay I will stay. Your people will be my people (even those with furry black hats) and your God my God."
Book of Ruth (1:16...not the furry black hat part)

Table of Contents

In the Beginning

October 2011:

This Shabbos (Sabbath) my husband, and I are celebrating our twenty-fifth wedding anniversary. Seriously! We were married during Parasha Beresheit (Genesis:1). We were sort of like the big bang, big explosion. Our wedding was eighteen days after Mordechai's birthday, eighteen days before my birthday and on the eighteenth of October. If you are new to Jewish numerology, eighteen represents "chai" (life)! To this day, Mordechai likes numbers so much that he assigns or looks for significant numbers in everything...odometers, house numbers, combination locks, etc. For example, he stopped me the other day from setting the microwave to thirty seconds. I was asked to set it to thirty-six seconds (double "chai"). Sure, dear, whatever you want. Anyway, whether you're into numerology or not, I'd say twenty-five years is significant. Whew! That is a long time in my book, and, yet, I wonder where the time has gone. Four kids, three dogs, four birds, a turtle and too many fish to count, here we are.

Here is a photo of my husband when we got married. He has that Don Johnson look going on!

And, here is a photo of him now. He's got that Don Johnson turned Hasidic rebbe thing going on.

There is quite a story behind all of this change, but let's just say a million dollar bet sealed our fate to be married, and a dream took us on this wild religious ride...and the rest of that story, you will need to read as you flip the pages ahead, if you dare. Well, here's to great beginnings, our journey, a deep appreciation and to many more meaningful years. I did promise him I wouldn't get another dachshund in the next twenty-five. Instead, I told him I'm getting two. Looks like someone's going to get kicked out of the bed!

Introduction

Living
With a conscious effort
To connect
To a higher source
Our paths linked together
Destinies unknown
Yours I must accept
Mine you do not own
Cover me
Contain me
Direct me
Destroy me
Yet like a tree
Grows its own way
That bends
Only with the strongest of wind
Or ice...holds firm and then
Very slowly
...it melts
Losing its beauty, purpose and form
From the intimidating warm
Yet I am who I am
Deeper than skin
See me
Hear me
Love me
Know me
Then my life...will begin

I am a Jew. Some would refer to me as an Orthodox Jew, others perhaps not. I am also a mother, daughter, sister, aunt, friend, and wife. I am no ordinary wife. I am the wife of a Hasidic, Orthodox Jewish man. I often think of myself as an army wife. I have not always lived this way. Someone recently asked me, "So how long have you been Orthodox?" I really couldn't answer. There is no single point of change. My becoming Orthodox has been a process. I did not intend to be an Orthodox Jew and I may not be what you would traditionally call an army wife. My husband does not serve in the United States army, Israeli army or any other country's army. He signed up to live as an Orthodox Jewish man, for God's army.

He just forgot to tell me. Oops.

As his wife, my life changed as well. There is no way I could have imagined what my life would look like today or the outcomes of his decision and, thus, my own decisions. I can tell you that I am truly blessed and that God's hand has been in my life every step of the way; but, like many others, I didn't always see this part of my life that way. In fact, for a very long time, I felt cheated and robbed of the notion of what my life "should be like."

It is ironic, yet divine, that I would find myself as an army wife. Like others, I have danced between several roles while trying to get to know myself. As a Jew, I have been categorized as Conservative, Orthodox, Modern-Orthodox, and "we can't really figure her out." I would often tell people that I am Re-Frum. That pretty much covers all labels from Reform to Frum (religious). I don't like labels, but people seem to need them. I prefer to break them down and dance in and out of them scooping up bits and pieces of all of them. Labels create definition for both the labeler and the labeled. The two perceptions often do not meet. But, perhaps if you think you know what I am, then perhaps you can feel more secure in knowing who you are. My dislike for labels says a lot about me as well. It is an aversion to commitment and critique. It is much easier to be diplomatic. Everyone is happy that way...at least for a while. I learned at a very young age to minimize conflict and have avoided it much of my life, or, perhaps, it's just the way I'm wired. Conflict, arguments or a heated discussion can send me down to my knees or at least to a corner with a stomachache. In taking extreme means to avoid conflict, I have sometimes lost myself and even gone as so far as to sabotage myself. There is a price to be paid for that.

I was not raised as an Orthodox Jew, but I have lived an observant lifestyle, and to some an extremely observant lifestyle, now for over sixteen-plus years. Sometimes I have lived that life with integrity and sometimes as an excuse, while secretly sucking up anything and everything spiritually tantalizing that may or may not fit the definitions of Orthodoxy. At the heart of it all, I yearn to search for the divine. Somehow, while trying my hardest to avoid organized religion, I found myself being raised in a traditional, religious, Jewish household and then married to an Orthodox man. Go figure.

Like many others who have returned to Orthodoxy, I am frequently labeled as a "Baal-Teshuva" or "BT" (one who has "returned"). You really have to be a bit crazy, or married to someone a bit crazy, to take on this label. Being a BT implies that one has returned to our intended purpose here, to our soul work. It describes Jews who have chosen to become observant of Torah mitzvot (commandments) but even more so, it describes Jews who have returned to God's purpose for us here. For most of my observant life, I was truly not deserving of such a label, as I was a "closet rebel," secretly doing things like tearing toilet paper on Shabbos (a big "no-no"). Today, I believe I am beginning to wear the label of Baal-Teshuva proudly. I've thought of sewing it into the back of my shirt. In my own searching, I have found that although we are all on a journey "home," there are times (at least for myself) that I have been lost, feeling that I was perhaps deserving of something different, better or easier. It is easy to fall off this path or just get stuck in one spot. And, there have been times in this journey when I couldn't help myself from sometimes wondering if Orthodoxy was the path for me or whether I was capable of living an Orthodox life. Becoming an Orthodox Jew is not just hard, sometimes it's....annoying! And, yes, sometimes it's extremely joyful. Yet, it requires intensive study, hard work and change. It is advanced work, and not everyone has the drive to be observant; for at its very foundation, Orthodoxy is a service to God based on the laws and ethics of the Torah. It is army service. Don't think you're in God's army? I didn't either. I would often whine to my husband, "I don't want to be on the front lines." But, I was. I am. And, like any soldier on the front lines, I needed training.

If lived with the right intention, Orthodoxy can elevate the soul. It is authentic, rich, secure, spiritually tantalizing and most importantly it opens a door to a relationship with God and an understanding to our purpose here. What may seem to an outsider as chauvinistic, old-world or degrading, can be a life lived with divine balance. All those strange and seemingly obsessive rituals actually create a cosmic balance between left and right, man and woman, day and night, light and dark, physical and spiritual, if they are done with the proper intention. Observant Judaism can be a path to holiness, which is not left up to the definition of culture, emotion, nature, whim, personal preference, what "feels right" or even love in the traditional sense. It can, however, provide the music and backdrop for a slow dance with God. And, although some of us may be stepping over our own two feet, we can all learn to dance, even gracefully.

In living an Orthodox lifestyle I have had to dig deep within myself, to stretch myself and to contain myself against my nature. It is hard. As a good friend of mine said, "I got the rest of eternity to be spiritual. I'm not going to waste my time here doing that." But, Orthodoxy teaches that the here and now is training for eternity. It is this living above and beyond nature that prepares us. As Orthodox Jews, we take something very natural, such as intimacy, and we put restraints and boundaries around it, taking it beyond what may seem instinctual, in order to make it holy. For me, that has been a struggle and at times very uncomfortable, if not down right

10

scary. We live in a society where lack of restraint, freedom of expression and nonconformity is of value, not restraint or commitment. We have come to believe that everyone is equal and deserving. It is not so in Orthodoxy, where the goal is for everyone to be respected as a unique soul but with a specific divine purpose.

In addition, Orthodox observance requires "handle with care." It can backfire on those who are not spiritually intact. It is like trying to learn calculus without knowing how to add. If you think of your soul as a hard drive on a computer, then installing software in the form of commandments can either boost up a strong hard drive or wear down a weak one. For those who come into Orthodoxy with their emotions, heart, soul and minds running a super hard drive, the software that is installed can be, let's just say, wow! Otherwise, well, you have your work cut out for you, and as I have found out, it's an uphill climb. Some of us need to learn how to be human beings before we can become spiritual beings.

My story is an awakening, an education, a journey and, yes, sometimes, well, a comedy. I have centered much of this story on my husband, but, the truth is, it is a story of my own journey where he is often my messenger and, as hard as it was for me to imagine at times, indeed my soul mate.

Why write my story now? For so many years I was defining myself by my role as a physical therapist, catalog director, mother or wife. I never really thought about my role as a Jew. I initially began writing my blog, *Married to a Yid*, for myself, as a cathartic response to becoming Orthodox. I found out that I was not alone. Readers of my blog were eager to see what sort of mess I was getting myself into and laughing with me all the way. I began this book as a gift to my husband and to further explain my intentions to myself. And, although my husband, Mordechai, does provide the material and personality for making a great story and blog, I was hiding out behind my sarcasm. For eighteen years, I built up a career that I thought was my identity. When I left the corporate world, I began to wonder who I was. I began to question my identity. Who was I without my title, my thoughts, my body or my senses. What was my soul? My purpose? What about the things I had accomplished? Were they of value? What about the things I had done wrong? What was their cost? As time rolled along, this book became a dedication to a much higher purpose. It became a dedication to my journey, to those whose lives I might be as so humble as to impact and ultimately to God.

We all have a purpose here. It comes from an Almighty source of love. Rabbi Shlomo Carlebach once explained that the difference between Abraham and others who worshipped God was that Abraham not only taught the world that there was one God, but he taught the world that God loves us. If you are loved, really loved, then how can you *not* be committed to the one who loves you?

Some days I know what my purpose is and other days I wonder. Like everyone, there are times I struggle and I have detoured far off my path. Those struggles have taken me to some incredible low places and some amazing highs. I am still learning, growing and discovering. Perhaps, you are too. If we are not searching, if we don't look within, then we are not living. Sometimes the struggle is downright painful. Sometimes we blame others. Sometimes we are the source of someone else's misery. Ouch. Sometimes we dance with joy and sometimes we are just plain scared. All of this is part of living.

Here is my story. I hope it makes you think, laugh and love. I share my story to shed light, give hope and show value, joy and commitment to our families, our communities, our spouses and ultimately to the divine within us. Ultimately that has been my struggle and my lesson to learn: that commitment is a form of love, and integrity and gratitude are at its foundation.

Dedication

It is with extreme gratitude toward God and all that He touches, including my parents, siblings, in-laws, children, nieces, nephews, community, friends and most importantly to my husband, Mordechai, that I dedicate this book.

And to you:

May you find joy and meaning in this world. May you be a source of holiness and joy for all those around you. May your life here be a successful one. If you should happen to be lost, know that you are not alone. May you find your way, ultimately back to God. There is a map if you need one. Have a safe and meaningful journey.

Ilana M. Danneman

P.S. This book contains quite a few Yiddish and Hebrew transliterated words. There is a glossary in the back to further explain their meanings (and give you a laugh). In addition, this book references God, the Almighty, the creator many times over, so, please be cautious where you leave your book. And, *please* sneeze in the other direction! Gezundheit (see glossary)! You will be good with the commandment "do not destroy God's name (Deutoronomy 12:4)." Whew! You can relax now.

The Hand of God

Rabbi Zusha used to say: "When I die and come before the heavenly court, if they ask me, 'Zusha, why were you not Abraham?' I'll say that I didn't have Abraham's intellectual abilities. If they say, 'Why were you not Moses?' I'll say I didn't have Moses' leadership abilities. For every such question, I'll have an answer. But if they say, 'Zusha, why were you not Zusha?' for that, I'll have no answer."

In the Beginning

I am in the third grade working on a spelling assignment. A little boy is leaning over my shoulder.

He is bothering me.

Little do I know that this is the boy I will someday marry. My school, the Hebrew Academy, is the only Jewish day school in Atlanta in 1972. There are two hallways, a lunchroom/auditorium and office area. There is one secretary who types, answers phone calls and puts Band-Aids on kids, all at the same time. There are eighteen students in our class, and we call roll by announcing our last names. This year our third grade is somewhat of an experiment. We have an "open" classroom. There are no permanent walls, just those temporary, flimsy ones that if you lean on, the bottom moves. We can always hear when other kids are in the hall. The lack of permanent walls is supposed to create an open learning environment. The idea behind this is that we are to create our own structure. We are given assignments at the beginning of the week to work on daily and to be turned in by the end of that week. At eight-years old, this works for some of us and for some of us, well, it doesn't. Our teacher's name is Mrs. Falik. Enough said. She can raise one eyebrow while glaring down at you. Mrs. Falik's eyebrow and the fact that my mother works in the school (as the kindergarten Judaics teacher) is enough to make me complete my weekly assignments. It doesn't work too well for others, though, and that eyebrow goes up a lot in our third grade class.

Today I am paired up with Michael Danneman to work on spelling. He is tiny, like me, with beady little brown eyes and straight, brown hair. I have big, blue eyes and curly hair. Our size is about the only thing we have in common. He is one of the people for whom the lack of structure doesn't work so well, and he rarely has his homework done. So he gets "the eyebrow" a lot. Anyway, I am not too pleased to have to work with a boy, much less a boy who needs the eyebrow to do his work. In addition, I just want to get my assignment completed and turned in quickly. This will be one of my struggles for most of my life: quality versus efficiency. I am organized and efficient, not detailed. Details annoy me.

FOR MORDECHAI, EVEN SPELLING WAS SACRED – YOU COULD NEVER ADD NOR DELETE EVEN **ONE** LETTER...

We are assigned to work on a spelling assignment. Michael leans over my shoulder and with as much condescendence as

16

an eight-year-old can muster up says, "That is NOT how you spell 'between.' You are missing one 'e'." I am now for sure regretting having to work with a boy, much less this eyebrow-deserving-know-it-all. I reply, "Yes it is! That *is* how you spell between, b-e-t-w-e-n." He says, "Let's make a bet." I say, "Okay, I'll bet you a million dollars." He ups the bet to five million, and we agree. Little do I know that this bet will determine my fate and change my life. I have just had one of my first lessons in why it is dangerous to say "yes" when you really mean "no," another lesson that will repeat itself over and over again. Our assistant teacher, Mrs. S. settles our bet. Michael wins. It seems that I not only lost one "e" when spelling "between," but I also lost five million dollars *and* my pride. To this day I do not spell too well nor have I paid back the five million dollars, at least not in the fiscal sense.

Both of Michael's parents worked until five o'clock. It was Michael's routine to call his mother every day after school when he got home. The day of our bet, he was so excited and talking so fast that she couldn't understand what he was saying. "Mom! I'm a millionaire, I'm a millionaire! His mom said she couldn't wait to hear about it. When she arrived home, she was greeted at the door with the same enthusiastic "I'm a millionaire, I'm a millionaire! I bet Ilana Maslia five million dollars and I won and now I'm a millionaire!" His mother looked him straight in the eye and said, "The only way you will ever get that money is to marry her." And so, the prophecy was set and my fate was sealed. Years later Mordechai (aka Michael) would remind me of this bet at various times. He loves to tell this story as to him it was not so much about the five million dollars as it was about the power of words and the hand-of-God in our everyday lives.

Growing Up Jewish

I grew up in a fairly traditional Jewish household, and the only way I know to describe my upbringing is to say that we were "Conservative-Sephardic-Ashkenazi-Traditional" Jews. This meant we kept a kosher home, ate burekas and matzah balls...and celebrated most holidays. We were not observant. We were committed, though. There were no kosher restaurants to be found in the sixties and seventies in Atlanta, yet even if there were, I'm not sure whether we would have made them our only choice. Like many kids growing up in the thirties and forties my own parents were assimilated into American culture and so were we. So growing up, we were religious, non-kosher-restaurant-goers, for even though we would eat a hamburger at just about any restaurant, we would NEVER, eat a cheeseburger. It all had something to do with a mother goat, her milk and her baby (Exodus:23:19) and the fact that my mother's mother kept kosher. What I didn't realize at the time was that keeping kosher was so much more than a dietary restriction. A dietary restriction constrains what someone eats. Kashrut determines not only what we eat (no pig, no bugs, no meat and milk together and so on), but how it is cooked, what it is cooked in, who cooked it and at its highest level, your intention upon eating. It is a way of feeding the soul, not a diet for the body. And, I can surely tell you, from some of foods that are labeled as kosher, or the foods cooked in a typical Jewish home, it is not about the body. One can for sure be healthy and keep kosher, but one can also eat like, well, a pig and keep kosher as well.

My family always celebrated the Sabbath, aka Shabbos, aka Shabbat (as I was taught with the Sephardic pronunciation) every Friday night. As soon as my mother came home from teaching kindergarten on Friday afternoons, she would begin preparing a delicious meal with aromas that would waft through the house. At 7:00 sharp, we began our Shabbat meal. We sang the traditional song that welcomes the Sabbath, Shalom Aleichem, my father recited the Kiddush (blessing over

18

the wine), we said the Hamotze (blessing over bread), ate a deliciously prepared meal and finished it off with an abridged version of the Birkat (blessing after meals). We were observant from our perspective. I then ran off to watch television. The Brady Bunch was my favorite show, and it aired at 8:00p.m., so I was in front of the TV by then, religiously.

We celebrated every Jewish holiday including building a sukkah to celebrate Sukkot. This involved constructing a "hut" that commemorates the clouds of glory that protected the Jewish people when they travelled through the desert. It represents God's protection and our faith in Him. As a kid, it was a cool place to hang out for a week, and I loved watching my dad suspend the structure from the outside corner of our house. It raised a lot of talk amongst our Jewish neighbors. They considered us very "religious." Looking back, I'm not sure why my parents picked up the traditions they observed. I don't remember a lot of discussions about why we did what we did. They both had a yearning for Israel and for Jewish traditions, which they felt was crucial to pass along. Why? As Tevya said in the Fiddler on the Roof, "Tradition!" It was how they were raised. Either way, it was clearly important to them, and, in spite of their day-to-day stresses, they took the time and made Jewish education and observances a part of our lives.

We attended a Sephardic (Jews originating from the Iberian Peninsula: Portugal and Spain) synagogue, Or Ve Shalom that was also Conservative, which is somewhat of an oxymoron, as typically Sephardic Jews are identified as being observant. Our synagogue was more Traditional-Conservative. It was too observant for Conservative Jews but too Conservative for Orthodox Jews. No one that I was aware of at our synagogue, other than our beloved rabbi, was completely observant. The custom that received the most attention at Or Ve Shalom was cooking and eating burekas. To this day, the burekas draw almost as much attention as the high holidays. We all pined for them like we should have been pining for God. This "kehila" (literally: community) was the community center for my father's side of the family. His siblings, cousins and all their offspring along with many other Sephardic Jews attended services there. It was like one big, happy, bureka-loving family. I still love to visit the Or Ve Shalom. It still feels like home and I don't mind the burkeas either. But, unlike the other kids at our synagogue, we also attended Jewish day school. It was my mother who insisted on this. It was at the Hebrew Academy where I learned the joy of holidays, mainly through singing. We had great music teachers, one of whom brought her guitar "George" along to each class, making us clap and sing along with her. My mother also insisted, after living for four years in Israel prior to my birth, on providing me and my older sister, Alisa, with Hebrew names as our only names, and sending all four of her children to Jewish day school at any cost. To this day, I value those parts of my upbringing beyond any measure.

It was all these experiences, traditions and love for Israel that formed my understanding of being Jewish with the addition of one more significantly important influence. My spirituality was something I, no doubt, found by spending four weeks of every summer at overnight camp in the North Georgia Mountains. My summers at Camp Barney Medintz, where the entrance states "Every Child Makes Himself Known By His Own Doings," created some of my fondest memories. I found Camp Barney to be my first touch with myself, with nature and what I knew to be spiritual. As I look back at the time I spent in that special summer place, I simply cannot replicate it nor put a price tag on my memories. To this day, I can close my eyes and be transported back. I honestly believe there is a spiritual vortex there and I don't think I'm alone. Truthfully, Camp Barney was family, and it offered me the security to just be. I didn't need religion. I had camp, a very special camp. Although it was a Jewish camp, I heard no one speak directly of God at camp; yet, I felt closer to God at camp than I did anywhere else.

The only person I heard regularly reference God during my youth, was our rabbi, as he referred to the "Almighty" in his

20

sermons. But, with his heavy French-North African accent and my lack of motivation to being in synagogue, I certainly didn't hear much. I remember learning about Torah and mitzvot, but they seemed more like another subject. It seemed as if the word "God" was a bit taboo. It belonged to religious freaks, weird people. I surely never knew what it meant to be "created in the image of God." If I thought about God, I thought about blue skies, trees and lakes.

After attending the Hebrew Academy, I attended a year of public school in the eighth grade where I was exposed to drugs, cigarettes and kids with less than stellar habits. It was very *educational*. At that time, high school went from eighth through twelfth grades. Since I had a late birthday, in reference to my peers, I was a twelve-year-old who looked nine, going to school with eighteen-year-olds who looked twenty-one. My oldest sister, Sheryl, decided that I was not in a good place and suggested to my mother that she find me another school. And, so she did. Without the resources to do so, somehow my mother managed to find a way to send me to Yeshiva High School. There I was exposed to a difficult dual curriculum of Torah and secular subjects. My favorite was French. I had no intention of being observant. I saw no reason to be. In my mind, the study of Torah was just a subject, and the teachers of Torah were "those Orthodox people."

So, growing up, my Judaism encompassed a lot of fun with just a few restrictions. My perception is a credit to my parents, the Hebrew Academy and Camp Barney Medintz, all of whom showed me the joy of being Jewish. I like to think of the Judaism that I experienced as public transportation Judaism. You get on when you want and you get off when you want. I am not belittling the effort (from my parents or any of the institutions) or their own pure intentions, much of which registered loudly and clearly to me. To this day, I am thankful for all they gave me. I am just suggesting that it seemed like our Judaism was more of a choice and not an obligation.

I loathed rules, the idea of praying, standing still or thinking about the Torah. My mother loved the synagogue. She loved singing all the songs. She would stand next to me and ask me to sing louder. So, I did. I despised having to put on nice clothes and going to synagogue. In fact, my favorite day was Saturday when I could watch cartoons, run around in cut-off shorts and my camp T-shirt, ride my bike and climb trees. There were years when we did not regularly attend synagogue on Saturday. During those years, my mother bought me two dresses each year: one for Rosh Hashanah and one for Pesach (Passover). They were the only two dresses I would wear each year and only one time each. If anyone told me that I would be wearing skirts seven days a week when I got older, I would have thought they were on drugs.

On My Own

I left my home at age seventeen, after twelve years of Jewish day schools, nine years of Jewish camp and a love for matzah ball soup and burekas, and headed off to college with $25.00 in my pocket, to become "financially independent." It never occurred to me that perhaps I was lacking a relationship with God. I didn't realize I needed one.

My financial independence goal and several part time jobs drove me through four years of college and kept me out of most trouble, yet spiritually, I wasn't prepared. I really did not know what my values were, and I was not prepared to defend the few that I thought I had. I was like a leaf blowing in the wind, landing and experiencing whatever came my way. As the fourth child in my family, I was a follower when it came to family and religious values. Had anyone asked me to delve deeply into myself to see what I wanted from my life, I would have been baffled if not annoyed by the request.

In June of 1986, I reached my milestone of independence. I graduated college and went on to my first job as a physical therapist. I was proud of my professional title. I was content with my professional direction and definition.

Our Early Years Together

My husband, Mordechai, grew up in a secular family. If anyone deserves a reward for insisting on a Jewish education for their children, it would be Mordechai's mother, who aware of her own lack of Jewish knowledge insisted on sending her two boys to Jewish day school. In 1972 that was no small feat. Michael spent his summers in Canton, about an hour north of Atlanta, working on his grandmother's farm. He learned how to farm, grow vegetables, can salsa, shell peas, make homemade ice cream and play cards. All of this would form family values and a work ethic that would stick with him throughout his life. He would be exposed to some of the major Jewish holidays, but only through friends and day school would he learn about living like an observing Jew. Yet, even as a small boy, he would ask his father to take him to the synagogue on Saturday mornings. To this day, as a child who found every reason to avoid going to synagogue and whose mother had to practically feed me candy intravenously to keep me still while in synagogue, the idea of asking to go to synagogue, especially at such a young age baffles me. This alone should have alerted me that I was not dating a "normal" Jewish person, but someone on a religious journey. But, it was not just his yearning to go to synagogue, it was his constant obsession with religious people, books on the Torah and Torah study. I just had no idea what was percolating deep down inside of him and I'm not sure he did either.

Mordechai, well *Michael* as I knew him at the time, asked me to marry him on May 6, 1987 in a park. He picked me up in a limousine and had a blanket with strawberries and champagne waiting. His brother was hiding in the bushes videotaping his proposal. His charm, attention to detail and

23

"production-style" personality was dizzying if not endearing. I said, "Yes!" We were not so unique in that our early marital years were difficult. The fact that we stayed married in spite of our early differences was nothing short of miraculous. Even our beloved rabbi would often remark that the Dannemans "define diversity." His observations were right on the mark, and I think we often baffled him. I would, occasionally, pay him a visit with tears in my eyes. "I just can't keep up with him," I would complain. Our rabbi would look at me, say something nice and understanding and watch me walk out the door, probably baffled himself and wondering how he had attracted such strange, unique and confused people into his community. I think if he had kept a list of "potential success stories," we would have *not* made the cut.

Marriage is a connecting of two souls to form a more complete whole. That may or may not always "feel" good. Sometimes our spouse points out to us what we're missing. It is not always what we *want* to see. But, it may be what we need to see. Yet, this bending and flexing to adopt and accept what often feels so strange has, at least from my view, taken me to levels I could not have ever reached on my own.

During our first week of marriage, Michael looked at me one evening and said, "You don't really believe in God, do you?" If there was one pivotal moment in my life, that was it. It is not that God and I had such an intimate close relationship. Other than saying Shema (centerpiece of Jewish prayer) before bedtime and asking for good-grades (At least I had my priorities straight!), I hadn't really talked much to God. I really wasn't sure if God really cared whether I believed in him or not. I really didn't think my opinion of God mattered much.

At any rate, who was this person standing across from me accusing me of not believing in God? My response was, "Huh?" I would give him that response many more times throughout our marriage. "Where is all this coming from?" I asked. He replied, "Well, if you did really believe, you would be keeping all the mitzvot (mitzvahs) in the Torah." The Torah? What did that have to do with anything?

Looking back, I really didn't know who I was. Michael asked me why I kept kosher. At the time, we kept kosher at home, although we ate non-kosher food in restaurants and other people's homes. I told him I kept kosher because my grandmother kept kosher and my mother kept kosher. He explained that unless there was a divine element in each thing we did, it had no purpose or lasting value. The funny thing was that Michael really valued the level of Judaism that my family embraced. It was one of the things that attracted him to me. He was taken and impressed by the fact that we kept kosher, celebrated Shabbat and built a sukkah.

My explanation on kashrut seemed to me to be a very honest and valuable explanation. To Michael, though, as he explained, my reasoning was simply not solid enough or strong enough to hold up for very long. One more generation and it would dissipate, unless you had a better reason, unless the Torah was your reason. I simply was not ready to grapple with this idea at the cost of losing my footing on how and why I had lived my life for the past twenty-two years. I didn't think that way.

I was having visions of his having a lobotomy.

One thing I've learned about my husband is that he is extremely persistent and does not give up easily. I found myself on a religious battlefield and didn't know why. I was not prepared for it at all. I decided that no good was coming of my current situation with its broken down communication, which I was for sure a part of. If my marriage was to work, I would have to give it my all. I either had to get out or get in. I was already in, so-to-speak, so I decided to give it my absolute best. I wanted to make this work. I could only be responsible for my own actions. I just couldn't figure my husband out yet. Each time I thought I knew his view on something, it changed.

As a young girl, I had many sleepovers with my friend who kept Shabbos. Her family was observant, and I would often spend the night with her on Friday nights, Erev Shabbos. Her family was warm and did not freak out when I accidentally turned on a light switch, which falls into one of the forbidden Shabbos tasks (thirty-nine prohibitions). Yet, all those Shabboses, in addition to a few spent at the home of a rabbi (and his family) in my high school did not motivate me to want to be observant. There were rules, routines, rituals, but it just didn't stir me. The idea of having rules in any part of my life was a deterrent to me. I did things that "felt" right not because someone said to do them. Too much structure was a clear "do not enter" sign for me and a "run for the nearest exit" warning. The people around me who lived more restricted lives seemed stuck. We respected the more observant Jews, but I got a distinct feeling that my mother felt insecure around them. Words like "the Orthodox" were a soft signal that something was not quite right with the "right" of us. My father was a shoe repairman in the only Orthodox community at the time. People would often bring him shoes an hour before Shabbat (Sephardic Jews say "Shabbat" whereas Ashkenazi Jews say "Shabbos") to have them fixed. He didn't look too kindly on that as he too wanted to leave to get home for Shabbat, and their assuming it didn't matter to him, did not sit too well with him. However, I remember him saying that Rabbi Feldman would bring his shoes to my father and say, "Please wait and fix them on Sunday." My father respected that. It showed a sense of respect not only toward the Torah, but also toward my father. These soft messages formed impressions for me. I understood early on that observant Jews were just people, some with great character and others perhaps lacking some of those traits.

So being observant, although not so foreign to me, was not a part of my making and not something I brought with me into my marriage. I brought family, holidays, music, singing, but not observance as an obligation. I vaguely remember one discussion when my soon-to-be husband asked me if I wanted to be religious. I remember my answer, "sure." Honestly, I thought "religious" could take on somewhat of a creative form. Plus, I didn't think he meant *really* religious. His definition of religious and my definition were not on the same side of anything. I saw religious as spiritual, you know, Shabbat in the park, a retreat in the woods, the Jewish side of "American Pie;" whereas, he saw it as observant of Torah mitzvot.

On our first date, Michael asked me if I was bothered by his kippah (Jewish head covering for men). I actually was touched by the question and loved the fact that he was struggling as to where and when to wear it. I also know that opposites attract, and as much as we would have a tug-o-war on a religious battlefield for many years, it was his adherence to black and white and my adherence to gray that would keep us yearning as we found our way, not only toward each other but toward a religious balance of conformity and individuality in our home.

On the anniversary of our first year of marriage, we headed off to Israel. We had hugs and kisses from our family. They were not sure whether we would stay or come back. We were on a program where we would spend three months on a kibbutz working and learning Hebrew and then the next nine months working in our professions in Israel.

During our year away, unbeknown to me, Michael would slip away to learn Torah. He immediately became a magnet to "men in black," black suits, black kippot and black hats. I just could not relate. Little did I know that not only was he learning Torah, but he was also learning how to scribe, which would eventually become a full time hobby, love and part-time job.

Heading Up

God works in mysterious ways and a couple years after our return from Israel, we were blessed with our first baby, a boy whom we named "Lev" (heart). What is really amazing about Lev's name is that, although we did not know it at the time, Lev was born on Rosh Chodesh (the first day of the month) Elul; and, there are several acronyms using the letters of the month that allude to love. One example is Ani L'dodi V'dodi Li (I am for my beloved, and my beloved is for me), which defines the Jewish people's relationship with God, their love for God and God's love for His people. Lev's name was a quiet message from God, divinely inspired. It would be the beginning of a long spiritual journey, for all of us, a journey away and back, to myself, and a search for God.

As I had grown up celebrating all the Jewish holidays, I wanted Lev to have the same real experiences. I asked Michael to build a sukkah. Looking back, this sukkah changed our lives. I never knew it then, but the sukkah, in all its beauty, simplicity and holiness, can be transforming. He really enjoyed building it, and we had our first real holiday as a family.

During this time, Michael was reading Torah at a Conservative synagogue. He was and is an excellent Ba'al Koreh (chanter of Torah). He learned this skill for his own bar mitzvah but then pushed himself to continue refining the skill. As a teenager, when other kids were going to movies and hanging out with friends, he was either studying or chanting the Torah. He would read every other week at the Jewish Home for seniors, spending two weeks learning each portion. In addition to reading from the Torah, Michael was now teaching bar mitzvah lessons, working as a respiratory therapist and secretly running off to study Gemara (interpretation of the Torah), sneaking it in whenever he could. I didn't really understand what he was learning or why. When I'd ask him, in not such an interested way but more of an accusing way, he would stop. A few weeks later he would start up again. When you're passionate about something, it just doesn't go away. At the same time, he also kept trying to start up businesses. None of them made it. The funniest one (or scariest) was when we invested $20,000 in specialized pool parts that would eliminate the need for chlorine in a swimming pool. We had an entire inventory and no business. He was convinced the business would "just come." I kept persuading him to make calls and eventually a large athletic club bought one. He nearly destroyed their entire pool system. I told him to take back the entire inventory. Immediately. He returned the inventory, got our money back in exchange for his pride. The pool business was done. God was still patiently waiting.

Then one day, he came home and said he was thinking of going back to school to be an anesthetist. Really? You mean we can talk about something else other than God, Torah and pool parts? I was thrilled. I was never scared of a challenge where I had to tighten a budget or get by. This one had the potential of a lucrative job at the end. And so, he applied, was accepted and enrolled in anesthesia school. I gave birth to our daughter, Carmelle, right as his program started. We were working hard with a bright future ahead of us. Michael excelled at his program, scoring the highest score *ever* in the history of the anesthesia board exam. I was beginning to realize how bright he was. He graduated with honors at the top of his class.

It was time to enroll Lev in a kindergarten, and we had to choose a school. We had both attended the Hebrew Academy and yet there was another Jewish school right around the corner from us. So, we went to visit Torah Day School. I was open to something different. The name was a little bit of a "put off" for me. I realized it was a religious school, but I honestly didn't realize how it would affect us as a family, or how it would affect Michael. The first day I went to visit the school, I showed up in a pair of jeans and a pink sweater. In religious terms, I looked like I had stepped out of the red light district. I didn't do this to be rebellious; it was just the way I normally dressed. The rabbi, aka principal, didn't flinch. He looked at me with the kindest of eyes, and I looked at him, and I said, "We are not observant. I'm not sure we will fit here." And, he said, "So many people claim they are not religious; 'observant' is a much better choice of words." I liked this man. He was probably the first religious man who I'd ever had a nice conversation with. I had never felt loved by a total stranger, but he seemed to be showing me love in a very respectful way, a different way. In addition, the school impressed me. The children stood up when we came into each classroom. I remember sensing that these kids had enough respect to have extra to hand out toward me. I barely had enough to fill my pink sweater. And, there was a feeling in the air. It felt new, different, with purpose. We enrolled Lev, bought him a pair of tzizit (fringes worn from the four corners of a garment) and a kippah and sent him off to kindergarten. We just forgot to tell him that his parents were a bit "off" from the other parents in the school. Lev didn't seem to mind.

A Tiny Shul

Meanwhile, the holidays rolled around again. Michael had just finished his anesthesia program and without my knowing slipped off to a tiny shul (synagogue) in Dunwoody, Georgia, not too far from where we lived. It seems like he kept having a repetitive dream ("I've had this dream thirty times!" he would claim) where he was led down a hall by a young boy into a glass shul. He told me about the dream several times, and I was sure he was slipping drugs and told him to go back to sleep. I was wondering why I hadn't followed through on that lobotomy. A few weeks later, while driving through Dunwoody, he saw a sign outside a house that read "Congregation Ariel." The day was Simchat Torah (a religious holiday) and he drove right up to the shul (a Sabbath prohibition), and walked in. As he entered the shul, he noticed something was different from other little shuls. The table that the Torah was placed on, the ark and the michitza (separates men from women) were all made from acrylic. They were clear, like glass. Ariel was the

30

shul from his dream! What was strange, he would later tell everyone many times over and over again, was that normally there would be, for example, a cover on a table where the Torah is placed. That day, as everyone danced around the table, the cover had fallen off, so the clear acrylic was even more apparent. He came home to me and told me he wanted me to come visit the shul in his dream. I knew for sure he was slipping drugs from the hospital, but was grateful at the same time to be a part of his excitement. I felt a change was imminent.

The shul was in a house. It was a ranch styled house that looked more like a drug drop-off, than a synagogue. The difference from our past synagogues to this one, was part of the appeal. We felt welcome right away, well, as welcome as a non-observant Jew can feel in a small house turned into an Orthodox shul. It was comfortable in an uncomfortable way. I felt out of place, yet like I was supposed to be there. We were invited to lunch where I sat across from the rabbi's two daughters, at the time twelve and thirteen. I was impressed. I had never seen tweens with such self-confidence and self-respect. Our two-year old daughter immediately fell in love with a lady that we named "Aunt Sandee." She climbed up into her lap the first day we were there. Now at nineteen, she'd still sit in her lap if she could. Ariel quickly became a home away from home for all of us. The warmth, the smell of cholent (soul stew) was palpable. Being a part of an Orthodox community was new for me, for us. It was warm, inviting, and I felt there was something more, yet I couldn't put my finger on it yet. Maybe it was that love feeling again. Even today, when I see a new face at our shul, I remember the day I first came to Ariel.

Michael told me that he didn't feel right having Lev in an Orthodox school when we were not observing the Sabbath and that maybe we should consider moving to a home walking distance from Ariel so we would not need to drive. His heart was set on this little shul from his dream. He also likes to tell people that there are two types of Jews: those who support the community and those that the community supports. He felt that if we moved to a bigger established community, we would blend in and not make such a difference. The community would support *us*. At Ariel we could grow *and* we could support the community. In addition, Ariel would give him a chance to lain (chant Torah) which he loved and so excelled at doing. It was a gift that he felt he needed to share. So, I thought about this and decided that walking to shul would be a nice "feeling." I was up for it. I just put down two criteria: One: He was NOT to go over the deep end. Two: I wanted a ranch style home, one story with a basement. He looked at me like a five-year-old whom you tell, "We're going to the pet shop to buy dog food...no pets." Then you walk out with a bird, a fish and a bunny. We found a home: three stories and he was so "deep" in the waters, I felt like I was treading to keep up.

One of the first things that changed was the day someone called our house and asked for "Mordechai," to which I replied, "Who?" It seems like he had started using his Hebrew name, Mordechai, but forgot to tell me. For such a smart man, he was often so forgetful. So, I asked him, "Did you change your name? Someone is on the phone asking for Mordechai?" For the next few years, I would introduce him as Mordechai to our synagogue friends and as Michael to our other friends as well as those who couldn't say the "chet" sound in his name.

In general, I was much slower at picking up religious observances for many reasons, but mainly, I just didn't buy into their necessity. I didn't have the "ah-ha" moment; no spiritual light bulb popped on and no burning bush was waiting for me. Honestly, had there been a burning bush, I would have freaked out and run. It was a slow, very slow, process for me. Even today, I honestly struggle with observance. I'm not a big fan of dogma. But, years of learning, thinking, pondering, meditating, praying and living in a community have taught me and inspired me well.

As I became observant, I decided to take on a mitzvah of going to the mikvah, a spiritual bath that women and men immerse themselves in for a variety of reasons. This is a beautiful mitzvah that can create spiritual and marital harmony. It is a rebirthing every month where man, woman and God are all part of the experience. It's like skinny-dipping with purpose. Initially, I had to "schlep" across town to a not-so-nice tank of water, dip, and return. After a while, I started to enjoy my little trips across town, for Delilah, the radio host of "Love Songs" entertained me on my trip there and back. I started to feel a real connection...with Delilah. In addition, the mikvah was upgraded to more of a "spa" experience. Eventually a mikvah was built for our community, Ariel, a beautiful mikvah. One visit in particular, though, sticks out in my mind. At that visit, my very holy attendant approached me and said, "How do you make water?" To which I wondered to myself, "Why do I keep attracting these strange people into my life who speak in code?" I dutifully replied "H_2O." She then looked me in the eye and said, "The details matter." It was her nice way of reminding me how important the mitzvah I was performing was and how crucial the details were. Details. To this day, they haunt me. It seemed like every mitzvah I took on was an uphill climb. Though, the details were like the hand and footholds on a rockclimb, I didn't always see them that way.

Climb Up

This week I went rock climbing. I have climbed many times over the past years, but I am still a novice, as I don't do it too often. It is not a very modest sport for an Orthodox woman, but then again I'm not your typical Orthodox woman. Rock Climbing takes agility, strength, endurance and focus...and is not done well in a skirt. This presents a challenge. I decide to ditch the skirt for the climb. Those climbing harnesses just don't work well with a skirt on.

So off to Stone Summit I go. I have watched experts and novices and most recently took six little boys, including my own, as a birthday celebration. I have also been certified to belay another person and have received some great climbing tips, such as not swinging on one foot (not very stable) and leaning toward the wall to maximize leverage. I am convinced as with many sports that there is a spiritual/emotional component that parallels the physical exertion and drive to climb...or not.

I recall many years ago getting stuck on Mt. Yonah in North Georgia. I was the last climber up a 300' climb and couldn't figure out how to go up. Yet, I couldn't go down either. I panicked. I had to talk myself into going up, as down was just not an option. I wanted to just "get off" the mountain, and that was simply not an option. So, up I went finding the smallest of crevices I could grab onto. When climbing, it is important to have firm footing, a good grasp, to stay focused on the present (don't' look down....back) and keep going up. Sure, you might slip, but you won't fall far. Yet, if you just sit in one spot, you won't go anywhere. The top is pretty awesome too, and even though your hands give you a good brace, it is your firm base, firm footing and strong legs that keep you moving up. You learn from your mistakes. You have to stay focused on the goal. If you are belaying someone, their life is literally in your hands. You can climb on your own, but it is risky and you will go further, take more risks and get higher with a partner. So, you see the parallel? If not, look harder and go try a climb. It will test who you think you are. Oh, and, by the way, I accidentally forgot my skirt at the gym...hmmm.

Mordechai was continuously studying Torah. He always had a book in front of him. He is also one of the smartest people I know, sometimes too smart for his own good. It actually baffles me. He is self-taught, self-driven and a self-made Yid. But, if you can imagine a ski boat with a not-so-great skier behind it, that was the image that always popped into my head when I thought about our journey. My husband was driving the ski boat at a very fast speed, and I was the not-so-great skier, just trying to hold on for dear life. Sometimes I did fall, and when I did, I would get a full mouth of water, so to speak. But, he would just circle the boat around and pick me back up. Not ever did he think of driving off without me.

Send Search-Party, I'm Lost

I frequently felt left behind. Michael had such a strong passion for this journey. There were times it felt as if the Torah was his mistress (You're going to the synagogue again? Tonight?), but again, looking back, this was more of my own lack of confidence in my own journey then anything he was doing right or wrong. I kept wondering if I was giving up too much of myself? But who was I? I really didn't know. Could he have been more sensitive, more understanding? Maybe. It might have made things easier. Maybe he could have been a bit less dogmatic, but that was his style and he was learning too.

The Road Left Behind

Your view so different than mine
Empathy is all mine can be for you
I cannot feel the road
So difficult for me to keep up
To stay
Jumping through hoops
My feet never touching down
Following the map you call divine
Yet my road had no direction
So we left it far behind
Yet I wonder where it went
Maybe my avoiding it not so divine
So where are you going?
When you get there
Will I be left behind?
And all the time
The sacrifice so great
For the road I left behind

I began to question my own role and motives in my life, in my family, in my religion. Was I being honest to myself, to God and to those around me? Why was I leading an observant lifestyle, and if I didn't, how would I live now? If my husband was leading this religious journey, where did I fit in and why was he so zealous about it? I had to realize that sometimes what I perceived as too much zealousness, control or structure was Mordechai's own issues, way of thinking and personality and had very little to do with Orthodoxy. Sometimes my resistance was just from the delivery and not the message itself. His wanting the food served a certain way, needing a perfect kugel or his reference to ultra religious Jews as "my people" were more of a reflection of his own insecurities or need to belong. Yet it would send me running away.

I would often have to remind him that we were in this together ("remember we're married?") as his modus operandi was to take off in his own direction and thus leave me to my own. For the first few years, I just tried to keep up (while digging my heels as hard as I could into the ground). Yet, sometimes I was digging in too hard. I soon began to understand that the choice to be a religious Jew and to make my marriage work really was mine. No one was holding me down or forcing me. So, I decided to take this mission seriously. In addition to all the love and support I received from our own congregation, rabbis and rebbetzen (married to a rabbi), I enrolled in a program through AISH, the Jewish Women's' Renaissance Project (JWRP) that offers women a chance to connect to Israel, to their Judaism and to themselves. This trip wasn't necessarily for already observing women. In fact, most of the woman who attend were non-observant. But, as I explained on my application, I was a "dysfunctional observant woman." I felt that if I was to continue down this path, I needed to connect, for myself, by myself.

Me, Israel and the JWRP

There are over ninety women from five different cities. We have come together on the trip of a lifetime sponsored by JWRP...Jewish Women's Renaissance Project....to learn, to grow, to experience, to see, to....change the world....one woman at a time. I am on a bus with fifty of the women. We take turns going to the front of the bus to "tell our story." How did we get here? What are our thoughts? What will we take home? Why did we come? So, we talk and we listen. I tell my story. The bus is silent. They are taken by my journey. This particular day we are on our way to Masada. We have already been to Tiberius, Tsfat, the Old City and parts of Jerusalem. We have heard talks on Lashon Hara (gossip), the Kabbalah of You and World

Perfect. You can smell the holiness in the land of Israel...it's in the air. Stress has been eliminated for us on this trip...no cooking, no cleaning, no carpooling, no e-mailing, no laundry, no kids, no whining....No MEN. We can think about ourselves.

When was the last time we did that? I cannot even remember. So we learn, and we absorb. We think about ourselves, our families, our communities, our country and our world. Can we really save the whole world? So many people have come before us, and because of them we are able to be in Israel. We feel them around us...their stories, their lives, their legacies. We are inspired. Our eyes and hearts are open. We meet soldiers. They tell us their stories. We listen and our hearts go out to them. They are protecting this country. They are protecting the world. We wonder....who are we as Jewish women? We are lifted, and we are inspired here. So many people have worked so hard to provide us with this experience. We need to show thanks to this country...so we do what any good woman would do. Given a spare moment, we shop. We are helping the Israeli economy. We are paying back. But, seriously, we have to ask ourselves how will we pay forward? How will we live our lives so that the next generation will merit to be in this land? We bring all this back and now...the work begins.

We all have the opportunity to learn through our experiences, our lives, and especially our mistakes. I decided to put my best self forward. I changed my outlook. This is my life. No more griping, no more self-pity (well, maybe just once in a while). It didn't happen instantly. Yes, there are many days when I falter and cry, but like a climb up Mt. Everest, sometimes feeling oxygen depleted, things began to improve, one step after the other (and sometimes three steps down). There were plenty of struggles, arguments, frustrations, but I held onto the rope. I observed people: Orthodox and not, Jewish and not, good marriages and bad ones. I found role models and hung onto my community for dear life. God sent me some great role models. My friend Kim says, "Marriage is tough. But, you put your marriage first. Always." With that said, losing your entire self in your marriage would be counterproductive to a good marriage, as well. A good marriage needs both people. I now know that my husband needed a partner, a full attentive, awake, committed, and conscious partner. I had to trust that God would help me along the way.

Hasidim believe that God is in EVERYTHING. They may not live up to that outlook at all times, and sometimes they might lose sight of God amongst all the directives; but that is their intention. For many of them, that is the only way they know how to think. As I see it, sometimes our brains get in the way of our true selves, or our souls. Rulebooks are not my weapons of choice, and yet I have come to appreciate the boundaries and respect their divine source. Some people are often amazed that I have chosen to share my life with a man who embraces a more extreme side of Orthodoxy. I believe that the lessons that I've learned would have found me in another form. In his book on Emunah (faith), Rabbi Arush (translated by Lazer Brody) says: "There is nobody that can better help you attain your soul correction on earth than your husband or wife." I have to agree.

Army Wife of A Yid

My husband has been called up to "active duty." He is in New York with "his people" (Hasidim). He is hitting the hot spots like Boro Park (Brooklyn), New Square and Monroe, just to name a few. This mission is for "soldiers" only and so I stayed home to wo"man" the home base during the Shavuot holiday and the upcoming Shabbos.

I anticipate my husband's return "home" from his active duty. He has called me during his "service" to tell me how excited he is to be with people who "look just like he does." I ask him if this is a new revelation? Our joke is whether he will wear black pants with a white shirt or a white shirt with black pants. But, he explains that there are subtle differences. I suppose. Anyway, I am sure there will be many stories, adventures, casualties and victories (new-found kosher establishments) and new rituals from his service.

I often berate myself for not being a soldier. I know he and many others would feel more comfortable if I were more soldier-like, but I am just not soldier material right now, and being an Orthodox Jew is an army-like service. It requires much study, discipline, commitment, practice and obsession all mixed in with an unyielding belief. It calls upon us even when we wish not to be called upon. My children often ask me what I am? Ashkenazi? Hassidic? Modern-Orthodox? Sephardic? My answer is always the same. I am Jewish. I don't like labels...except there is one I will wear...."army-wife."

I believe God has huge plans for me. He must. As much as I've avoided him, He keeps giving me more chances. I pray He will reveal those plans to me and that I will recognize the signs as I journey forward. I struggle and sometimes I'm downright afraid. What if I took the wrong turn? What if I've missed the boat? Mordechai has been extremely patient with me. Perhaps that is part of our lessons to learn, not only patience, but difference, commitment and love. I think that we come to this earth for really only one purpose: to share a divine love through our own unique selves. Sometimes the chatter in our heads and our past experiences get in the way of that mission. It takes commitment, sacrifice, hard work, patience, compassionate listening, humor and, sometimes, incredible strength. If you are blessed, you get to spend your life expressing that love with one other person who will challenge you to the very end.

What purpose is there in loving you?
If not for the growth of your soul?
What purpose has time had in directing us
In growing from young to old?
Do we meet each lifetime
With a purpose on hand?
Or are the realities in shadow
The focus we stand?
To truly live life
We have to touch souls
And awaken them inside.
Sometime we hide
Behind a fear that we face.
But deep within
A soul is in place.
Whether you can reach me
Or I can touch you
Is the challenge we face
Each day a new.
And with each life
Our souls grow stronger
And perhaps with each meeting
Our souls connect longer
But you can be sure
That in this life...my goal
Is to move you in a way
Recognizable ...to your soul

Our Royal Spirit Wear

"...Who am I to be brilliant, gorgeous, talented, fabulous? Actually, who are you not to be? You are a child of God.....We were born to make manifest the glory of God that is within us. It's not just in some of us; it's in everyone. And as we let our own light shine, we unconsciously give other people permission to do the same. ...." Marianne Williamson

Head Gear

I'm sitting in a chair getting fitted for a wig, or as Orthodox women call it, a "sheitel." Although I'm comfortable now wearing my pre-tied bandanas and scarves, I decide I need a nice coif for special occasions. Yet, I'm still trying to authentically figure out how I got here. I don't mean how my GPS got me here, but how I got here. I have great hair that has personality, body and curl. I love the way it feels after it's washed and softened with a good conditioner. It takes me thirty seconds to fix it each morning. My curly hair is a gift from my dad's Sephardic genes. Not one hair is straight, and it grows perpendicular to my scalp. My father has said to me on several occasions, "I don't know why you would cover your hair. It's so pretty." So, why am I here? Honestly, it's a combination of wanting to look good, fit in, and be good.

I've polled many Orthodox women as to why they wear a sheitel. Most give me the modesty answer. A few tell me they are observing the halacha, aka, Jewish law. Some don't even think about it. They just do it, because that's what observant women do. Many want to fit into their communities. One friend tells me that her sheitel feels like a "hug from God." I think it's more like a vice grip.

My curls revolt. They simply refuse to lie down. They want out!

As the band goes around my head, I can feel my curls yelling, "SOS!" Another friend tells me that her choice to cover her hair had "nothing to do with peer pressure." She says it's a "royal" feeling. As I sit here contemplating my new look, I know it has everything to do with peer pressure. Well, I'm just being honest. Who in the world would put hair on good hair without peer pressure? My "sheitel dresser" makes a quick call to her "provider." From the murmured conversation, I think her provider might be working undercover. She says; "I've got one here, and you've never seen any hair like this. I'm going to send you a few photos to see if you can match it, but you won't be able to. It's really unique."

Great. I'm an experiment.

My sheitel lady keeps me waiting (which I don't mind) while she and her provider are finding my perfect wig. I come back a couple weeks later to try on some samples. There are five. One makes me look like Lucille Ball. One makes me look like a tennis ball. One makes me look like a poodle. One looks like the sheitel worn by every other Orthodox woman. I tell this to my sheitel dresser. She agrees, but felt that she had to offer me the traditional sheitel choice. The one I like is a combination of straight and curly and looks easy to manage, but the cap is giving me an immediate head rush. My sheitel dresser says "Wow! You're good. You can really tell the difference in a cap." She tells me that the other ones had a "stretch cap." I tell her I need the super-super-stretch cap. I explain to her that my curls make me very sensitive. When I was a young girl, people would walk up to me and pet my curls. It drove me crazy having people touch my head. So, yes, my head is sensitive. I text my daughter a picture of myself in all five "doos." She likes number two and number four. I choose number five. I haven't shown my husband as I decide I'm going to surprise him, both by my look and the price. I figure it's worth at least two of his streimels (the furry-bird's-nest-looking hat that Hasidic Jewish men wear). I'm also accustomed to low maintenance hair, so I tell my sheitel dresser I can't have anything that requires too much work. She walks around spray bottling my new doo and I am thinking sheitels and low maintenance are an oxymoron. In addition, she explains to me the fees and maintenance required. I decide right then that I am going on YouTube to find out how to care for mine at home.

TELL ME AGAIN HOW YOU NOW CAN FOCUS ON MY "INNER BEAUTY."

To Hair or Not to Hair

I have new hair. It's not my hair. It's someone else's hair. Yes, I tried this a while back but I just couldn't do it, so I'm going for round two. Hey, a girl's gotta look good! I'm somewhat obsessed with the whole subject. It's just so strange to wear hair on your hair. It's like God gave you hair and you're saying, "Uh, I like this other hair better." The rules for hair covering come from the oral tradition; but really, don't you think it would have been much easier if it were written down? "Cover Thy Hair." No guessing, no wigs, just cover it up. Now we're all confused. Honestly, I don't think God cares. Seems kind of insulting snubbing his original for a remake.

And, now I have to take care of this extra hair. You see my own hair was wash, pick and go! This new hair is spray and scrunch. Yesterday I sprayed the entire right side of my face and nearly blinded myself with a stream of water. How do you scratch your scalp? Do you ignore it? If you scratch it, something is sure to fall out of place. And, forget about going out in the wind, rain or snow. You're doomed. Plus, I now need a PhD in wig care or a second mortgage to pay to take care of it. Orthodox Jews are obsessed with hair. We grow it, cover it, "don't" do this to it, and "don't" do that to it. I think it all comes from our being way overly analytical about....everything. It seems to be very "in" these days to wear wigs even if you're not observant (or living with hair loss). Dolly Parton wears a wig every day and has for the past fifty years. Just Google "wigs." There's a plethora of websites selling them and telling you how to take care of them; and, you can get them in any style, length and color. It's a multi million-dollar business.

The weird thing is that my new hair is sitting on my dresser on a styrofoam head. It kind of creeps me out. Sort of like a skeleton in your room. My sheitel lady told me to name my hair. Hmmm, let see... Oprah, Cher, Barbara... Baldy... She Who Must Not Be Named.... I don't know. I'm not feeling such a close personal relationship. I mean, I name my plants, fish, pets, even my car, but my wig? And, here's the thing... I got so many compliments. Maybe I was better off not wearing it and drawing less attention. Honestly, no one ever said anything to me when I just wore my own hair. Truthfully, I don't get all the excitement over my new hair. Why does a wig make everyone so emotional? Why is it the litmus test for observance? My own hair is a mix between an afro and a sponge and never really turned anyone on. No blowing-in-the-wind-hair or Vidal Sassoon hair...just tight curls that like a little air to breathe once in a while. Sometimes I miss my hair. Sometimes I just miss me. Maybe I'm just thinking this through all too much. All I know is my head is itching...from the hair... not the thinking. But, I do like the look!

By Jewish law, a married woman is required to cover her hair. This was one of the most challenging aspects of Orthodoxy to grasp. Although it is standard in every Orthodox community, how it is addressed varies from one to another. For myself, I have slowly grown into covering my hair. It was not something I could do all at once, so I took it on little by little, day-by-day, hair strand by hair strand, curl by curl. Those darn curls. They still pop out. Reasons for hair covering vary from woman to woman. I have no recollection of any relatives who covered their hair, nor photos. In fact, the photos I do have are of my Yiddish speaking grandmother and her two sisters posing at the beach in their swimsuits. My grandmother made strudel and gave me hot oatmeal in the mornings. I don't ever remember her being concerned with covering her hair or any part of her body. With that said, I will digress just a bit so as to let you get a fuller understanding of this law.

The Talmud (oral law) states that married Jewish women may not appear in public with their hair uncovered. This prohibition is described from a Torah law: "And the priest shall set the woman before the LORD, and let the hair of the woman's head go loose. (Numbers 5:18)" I'm thinking hair going loose is not such a bad idea. But, the point here is that her hair was tied up, most likely covered. The "loosening" or uncovering was degrading and a consequence to her less than stellar behavior. So, from this we understand that her marital status was made public by her covered or "tightened" hair.

Two levels of obligatory hair covering are then discussed in the Talmud: complete and partial covering. Partial coverage of the hair fulfills the more basic standards. This level is the one that the rabbis say is alluded to in the Torah. Complete coverage of the hair, though not mentioned in the Torah, is still necessary in order to satisfy the requirements of conduct deemed proper for a Jewish woman.

The most common of head coverings for women are the sheitel, snood (pre-tied scarf), tichel (scarf) or hat. Yet, some cover their sheitel with an additional hat and some go as far as to shave their heads and then cover them with both a sheitel and a scarf. Talk about a serious headache.

A good sheitel can cost $1500 to $3000 or more and taking care of it is not so easy either. And, as a new bride in many Orthodox circles, the groom's family is required to purchase her at least one if not two or three of them. Of course, you can get a cheap one on-line for $35.00, but duh...talk about a conversation-lashon-horah (gossip) starter. Covering hair with wigs is debated among authorities. Authorities such as, Rabbi Moshe Feinstein permitted it, and the Lubuvatcher Rebbe encouraged it, while some authorities forbid it.

And men?

Men are required as well to cover their heads with a kippah. Jewish law does not require wearing a hat; however, there are some rabbis, especially in Hasidic Judaism, who require a double head covering of a kippah and hat or tallit during prayer. For men, there are kippot in black felt, black leather, knit, satin, black hats and, of course, streimels. It still amazes me that, in a sea of black hats, those wearing them can see the differences and make note of that person's community and observance level. What should be making us the same and make us holy is sometimes used to determine our differences.

I struggle with that.

Hand Shakes

Friends of mine often ask me: "Is it really true that Jewish men don't shake hands with women?" After I explain to them that Orthodox Jews are not hygiene-phobic, but it is a Jewish law, I then get the next question: Why does Mr. Goldberg shake hands, but not Mr. Cohen? So, I came up with some rules:

I explain that it's all in the "head covering" and one should remember the following rules:
1. If you are a woman approaching a Jewish man, look at his head.
2. If he has nothing on his head, you can shake his hand.
3. If he has a satin or decorated kippah on his head (he has probably forgotten to take it off from cousin Jake's bar mitzvah at the Temple), you can shake his hand and give him a big hug.
4. If he has a knitted kippah of any size, wait to see if he extends his hand and if so, you can shake it.
5. If he is wearing a black velvet or felt kippah, DO NOT shake his hand, and,
6. If he is wearing a felt black kippah and/or black hat, white shirt, black pants, take four steps backward. He may have already placed himself behind a boulder-sized piece of furniture to avoid any possible contact in the first place.
7. If you extend your hand and he says, "I have a cold and I don't shake hands," he is politely trying not to embarrass you.
8. If you accidentally shake his hand, he may a) shake yours, b) freeze with a panic-look on his face or c)

explain that he does not shake hands. Do not take offense. He is simply dumbfounded and does not know what to do. His combat training has not prepared him for this. But, you can help him out. Ignore any weird grimaces and simply continue on with the conversation.

9. Last, remember, he is part of a religious "troop" who follow strict rules to maintain marital purity where the separation of the opposite sex actually promotes sensitivity and respect. In today's day and time, you may even find it refreshing. Chivalry does exist even if it's in a bit of an altered form. Remember, it is not that he does not respect you. He actually does. And, here's the icing on the cake: you will walk away germ free.

I think of all touchy topics in Orthodoxy, the one that is most sensitive (and most judged) is hair and head covering. Jews are moved by it, annoyed by it, enjoy it, hate it, embrace it and avoid it.

There is a discussion in the Torah that deals with taking "leftover women" from warring nations (Deutoronomy:23). It is explained that in order to take a "left-over woman" (not to be confused with left-over cattle) from a war, a man would need to first cut her nails and shave her head (make her look somewhat like a war victim). If in thirty days a man is still attracted to her (deep inner beauty), he can then marry her having truly fallen for her soul and not just her external features. Once again, we see the focus on hair. As our rabbi said, "It's the exodermic features that we are often discussing." We are either covering it or cutting it off. Hair is a big deal, to everyone, religious, Jewish, or not. My sister-in-law, for example, decided that her hair must be colored right before the high-holidays, as she said it so eloquently, "Surely I cannot pray with gray!" I totally get that.

At any rate, wearing hair on your hair puts you into the hierarchy of religious Jewish women. Not exactly sure how that came to be, but if you're wearing a sheitel you are in a different category. This often puts people who don't cover their hair on edge.

I know.

This might say a lot more than we'd like it to. I have seen many newly observant woman put on a sheitel long before they knew what they were getting into, only to have it backfire sending them and their coif into a deep depression.

Hair can also determine your social status. In religious settings, there is a social "cut-off" which determines with whom one might share a meal. The cut-off requires three obligations: 1) do you keep kosher? 2) are you Shabbos observant? ....AND the biggest one.....3) do you (the woman of the house) cover your hair? The hair covering seems to be the caveat that can initiate you into the club, no matter what you do with the rest of your life. You are then a shoe-in and can be privileged to have guests of the highest religious observance in your home. There is no inquiry into the person's attributes, behaviors, lifestyle, work habits or how they treat their spouse or children. There is an assumption that a person meeting the three criteria will indeed model great character traits, and often this is true; but, the bar is set by the status of one's hair or head.

If you search high and low into the depths of the Torah, Mishnah and Gemara you will actually find very little about hair in comparison to other topics. Yet, it has become the litmus test, the high bar, the judgment call as to whether someone is authentically observant. Jews of every denomination make an immediate judgment call when meeting someone for the first time (within two to three seconds) by what is or isn't on their head and how what is on their head is worn. I have friends who wear sheitels, who don't, who wear hats, who don't, who wear scarves, who don't, and I have yet to find it indicative of their character, morals or even their observance of other laws. It would be much better if we wore hats that had a scrolling sign that said, "I gossiped today," or "I fed the hungry today." Then we would really be able to know whom we were meeting. I have often pondered the focus toward hair and have swayed from respecting the laws around it, to total bewilderment as to how it can be such an obsession. Yet, I suppose if we weren't using hair as a social status, we would have found something else.

With all this said, head coverings are part of living life as an Orthodox Jew and done with the proper intention and respect can, as part of a dress code, enhance spiritual growth and transformation.

Dress Code

There is a saying from midrash (biblical stories) that God offered his Torah to many different groups of people. But, it was only the Jewish people who said: "Naaseh V'nishma" (we will do and then we will understand). I mean, "WHAT WERE WE THINKING?" For sure we had it backwards. Shouldn't we understand first? Shouldn't someone have said, "and exactly why will I be needing to purchase $1500 wigs again?" before we all agreed to this?

Where was our lawyer?

Apparently, as I entered into Orthodoxy, I wasn't alone in my skepticism and apparently Jewish law wasn't going to change just for me. I really didn't have time to understand the laws of head covering and modesty and the ones I knew were not putting me into my "happy" place. I had to jump in very quickly to keep family harmony and to present somewhat of a united front to our children who were quickly growing confused.

Any good army has a uniform, and as our rabbi would say, you wouldn't show up to see the president in flip-flops and a mini skirt. Surely the Creator of the Universe deserves even better. He has a point. Only thing is, it just feels so good to jump around in a pair of shorts and a tank top. I now keep my less-than-modest-wear to my own home and often to my bedroom, well, at least the kitchen, okay, maybe the backyard and driveway. I can crank up some great music and have a great time dancing around my house. But, when I walk out that door, I do so with reverence: to God, to the Jewish people, to my community, to my family and to myself. I just hope God likes tie dye and understands that on Tuesday's I have to go tap dancing.

When we first enlisted in our religious army, I kept a skirt in my car (part of the "dress code"). This way, if we popped into a kosher establishment, I could whip on my skirt. I could have practically been Clark Kent's replacement with my speed and agility. But, since there were no phone booths, it became easier to just keep my clothes on, and, so I broke down and wore skirts, below my knee (sometimes they would creep up if I had a great pair of leggings and boots to show off!). Anyway, I slowly adopted this dress code. It became apparent that this identification was important to living as an Orthodox Jew, so I committed myself to the dress code with a tinge of rebellion. It not only acts as a modesty-booster, but in addition, it helps us identify each other in a crowd. I can pinpoint an Orthodox women from across a crowded room as if I had a built in ortho-GPS.

Ortho Scan

I was scanned yesterday, not by an X-ray, not by a CT scan and not by an MRI and not by the checkout lady at the grocery. An "Ortho Scanner" scanned me: another Orthodox woman giving me the "once over." There I was at the Coca Cola museum in Atlanta with my two boys, and she was there with her husband and children. We noticed one another as the only Orthodox people in the crowd (we tend to stick out a bit, especially in mid July dressed in long sleeves and skirts below the knee). As I smiled at her, her eyes quickly scanned me. Her smile then came as an obligatory afterthought (you can tell these things). She sized me up immediately and walked off. Man! I didn't pass the test...again. I knew I should have worn my wig, pumps and gray skirt to chase my twin boys around the Coke museum! Poor thing. She missed out on my great personality under my trendy-comfy-ortho wear. I just can't help it. I'm a product of the sixties and seventies.

You've seen the scan before. Their eyes quickly go up and down your body before meeting your gaze. I'm sure I confused her as although I was covered head to toe, had on appropriate clothing, and was toting around little boys with payos (side locks), something was a bit "different." Maybe it was my cool corduroy leggings? Of course, I'm sure she's just not the social type, or maybe she's one of those New York transplants (sorry, no offense, as I do have great friends from New York:). But, let's assume for a minute she isn't missing a social chromosome, as I'm sure she has at least a few friends. Then, perhaps, all the halacha is a bit misplaced, or maybe she was too exhausted to smile back.

I do tend to confuse people. Not on purpose. They just can't always place me in a box with a label. I'm sure I did not meet her standards: sheitel (I had on a hat that day), stockings (I had on leggings), pretty shoes (I had on Toms boots). I recently read a great article about Orthodox Jewry. It pointed out that we are missing the boat and falling short of our mission. We are just too judgmental toward outsiders and even toward insiders (apparently I need to read the article myself!). Ya think? The funny thing is that we are supposed to be doing all these mitzvot to uplift our soul. We're the "soul experts," so we think. Yet, externals consume some of us. Seems like we have a lot of work to do, and I am thankful for all those of you, Orthodox or not, Jewish or not, who are doing it, because truth be told, many of you are hard at work and changing some misperceptions. I think, though, we should first eliminate the scan. Let's just use it to ward off danger, not other "members of the tribe." So, dress appropriately. There is good reason to do so. But, I think if your scanner is turned on, you need to at least wear sunglasses. I may just do so myself, as there's a lady I know who wears bright orange and pink. It's killing me!

I've always known there was an observant dress code. It's hard not to miss it. I just figured there had to be a specific commandment, like "Thou shalt cover thy hair and not let the bend in thy elbow or knee show." My husband and I were different enough, so I tried to close the gap by adhering to the more modest, Orthodox dress code. I wasn't forced by any means, but I felt it necessary, albeit not so authentic on my part. I later came to live up to my more modest way of dressing and understand some of the detriments to the way our society encourages exposure. I was told that I was God's princess and should be attractive but not attracting. I appreciated the fact that I had a chance to shine from within, but I had a lot of work to do. There were times that the dress was uplifting, but sometimes it became a deterrent. As my daughter would often say, "Mom, my elbows just aren't that sexy." I had to agree.

One side effect of my new dress code, was getting "bageled." Bageling is when a religious looking Jew is approached by a not-so-religious Jew who asks a Jewish question, like "Excuse me, but can you tell me if this wine is kosher enough to take to my daughter in law's house for our Pesach Seder?" This can occur almost anywhere but the most likely place is a grocery store in the kosher department. So, with my hair, elbows and knees covered, I became an instant "kosher shopping advisor" to any Jewish passerby in the grocery store.

Today it is very *cool*, temperature set aside, to dress modestly. There are websites for the chic at heart that will cover a woman from head to toe, leaving *everything to* the imagination. They even sell chic, yet modest swimwear, although I've never seen anyone "swim" in it. But, there is an upside: you can cut back on the sunscreen. Ain't no rays getting through all those layers of clothing.

My dress is typically something of bohemian-upscale: a cross between down to earth and not too religious but very comfortable. I won't say I exactly passed any uniform inspection, but I found my own way to adhere to halacha and yet have my own style. Nevertheless, the Orthodox dress code can vary depending on what community you live in or who your rabbi might be; but, in general, for women, it requires skirts below the knee and shirts that cover elbows and collar bones. There had to be a definitive line drawn somewhere and our wise sages decided that elbows, knees and collarbones were a serious turn-on.

The Skirt of Shame Shop

Our daughter's high school has a dress code. The guidelines require that girls wear skirts that are BELOW the knee. I have purchased the appropriate skirts for Carmelle to find them unworn and replaced by skirts that may have fit her when she was twelve. It appears to her that her kneecaps are much higher than the school sees them to be. You know those pictures that four-year olds draw where the legs are coming out of their heads? Now, put a skirt on those legs and that is about how she wears hers. We have warned her that if she doesn't abide by the dress code and meets up with consequences that she will need to deal with those on her own. On several occasions, she has been sent to the office to don the "skirt of shame" (her naming of the skirt which the school calls "the skirt of bad choices"). This is a less-than-attractive skirt that falls to her ankles and needs to be pinned up at the waist so as not to fall down.

Donning the skirt elicits SOS texting to me and to her father to come rescue her or to not send her back to school. I smile. My husband beats his chest. Today she again infuriated her teacher ("Mom; she screamed at me and I was forced to wear the skirt once again!") It seems, she thought that by wearing leggings, she could move her kneecaps even further up her thigh. Not only that, but she informed us that "all twelve skirts" were out today, being worn by other "offenders." As she said, "Mom, the skirt of shame shop was all sold out today." I am thinking that maybe wearing the "skirt of odor" might work, or maybe no skirt at all as a consequence. Or maybe, when there is an offense, the parent should come into school wearing a bikini or boxer shorts. I think this is just the age where you push your limits and test your boundaries knowing that your parents or teachers will put their foot down. One thing for sure, I am convinced that the skirt of shame is not working, except to provide a creative challenge to the girls and school staff.

The dress code contains other subtleties such as closed toe shoes. Even our desert living forefathers and foremothers wouldn't have passed the shoe code. And, don't even think about a pedicure. Personally, I'm not one for nail polish, but if you love the sleek look, keep it to your fingers or cover those toes. Toes are way too sexy. You will also need tights or stockings on your legs if you are stationed in a more right-winged battalion.

Also, the more observant, the blacker the clothing is. It seems that too much color can be flamboyant. Of course, in more modern environments you can see a variety of colors and clothing, but those in the rabbi and rebbetzin ranks generally stick to white shirts, black skirts, black pants, black coats, black kippot and black hats. This "un-rainbow" dress code is quite sobering at times, but the color is not necessarily lacking....it is reserved for the service of the heart. Plus, the black and white does create a uniform and any good army... has a uniform.

The Summer of the Traveling Suit

My son is eighteen and wants a suit, no, not an astronaut suit or a suit of armor, just a regular everyday man's suit. My husband is distraught. To him wearing a suit and tie is the equivalent to getting a tattoo or a nose ring. He sees the suit as an offensive replacement to the "bekesha" (long Hasidic coat); whereas, my son sees it as a necessary part of his wardrobe. I am very much in favor of the suit (although not my idea nor my suggestion) as I think there are times when a suit is absolutely necessary. But, I suppose this Hasidic lifestyle is working. Had we started our son wearing suits, he might have navigated his way to ripped clothing and skinny jeans. Now he's wearing suits and feeling a bit rebellious. Something is definitely working.

The upside to the black and white uniform is shopping for clothes for my husband: white shirt and black pants. No deviations. He has received quite a few birthday packages filled with black socks, white underwear, white shirts and black pants. I would often ask him, if he didn't want to add a little color to his wardrobe. He would reply, "When the temple is rebuilt, we can wear color." And, I would reply, "Maybe the temple will get rebuilt *if* you wear color." I secretly thought of washing his Mighty-Whitey-Under-Uniform with my colored items, just for fun. My mother-in-law also tried to add some color into our lives. She loved the color red. She would buy my husband and kids red shirts, hats, sweaters, etc. It took her a few years and she too caught onto the dress code, broke down and purchased white shirts. I know how she felt shopping around a rainbow of colored shirts and picking out....white. It's like buying white candy.

Black is Cool

We frequently invite guests to our home for a Shabbos meal. We also frequently invite our extended families, as well. This past Shabbos we invited our family. My boys asked as they do each week, "Are we having guests this week?" To which I replied, "Yes, THE family is coming (the whole "Ganza Mishpacha)." They squealed with delight at the thought of their grandparents, aunts and uncles coming over for a Shabbos seudah, or as is appropriate for this Sephardic crowd " a Shabbat dinner." Anyway, my family came dressed in their very best Shabbos tank tops and pinstriped shorts (we welcome any form of dress to our table). Soon after their arrival, my husband and son came home from shul (after a half mile walk in the heat) dressed in their bekeshas (long Hasidic coat) and Shabbos wear.

Our dinner was lively, as our extended family brings laughter, singing and joy. They are truly our best participants and most lively guests, giving a great showing to a Conservative Judaism upbringing. There is never a dull moment and for sure never a quiet one. My husband has learned that to wait for a moment of silence to begin the Kiddush or a d'var Torah would be like waiting to quiet the trumpeting of the swans, so he jumps in on top of conversations to get things rolling. It is a fend for yourself to get attention and to be heard, and we all are comfortable amongst the cacophony of love and laughter. At one point, the discussion of the heat and the heat index surfaces. My husband explains that wearing the long black bekesha is actually "cooler" in 100-degree weather than wearing shorts and a tank top. This quiets the table as we are all waiting for the scientific explanation behind this. He goes on to explain that when you wear cooler clothing, you actually expect to feel cool. But, when you wear a long black coat, you don't have such expectations, and so you are actually not as hot as one would think. "You see, when I walk around wearing a long black coat in the winter no one thinks about it. When I wear it in the summer, it is obvious that I am dressed up for Shabbos and am wearing it for God. Nothing will keep you cooler than that." To this explanation, my brother (with the engineering PhD) says, "So, if we wear shorts in the winter, we should be warm then?" My husband replies, "Yes, if God would want us to, we would be warm." This non-rational thinking quiets even the most talkative. This also leaves one pondering on whether God cares much at all about our dress as well as the sanity of my husband. Then again, perhaps the dress is not for God at all, but for us.

Dressing children in the ortho-uniform starts as young as age three. My younger boys have beautiful golden locks that cascade down the sides of their faces. Their locks glorify the commandment: "You shall not round the corners of your heads..." If you stand back, you will see that their hairstyle mimics the look of sheep or billy goats. Their hairstyle is in direct opposition to that of a warrior, where the sides of their heads are shaved and the top spiked. Jewish Hasidic boys cut the top short and grow the sides long. We are not warriors in the physical sense, but we are a flock; and, well, "the Lord *is* our shepherd." In addition, boys from age three and up are required to wear tzitzit, fringes that remind them, and all who can see them, of the 613 commandments. That is quite a toll for a three year old and a washing machine travesty for mothers.

Tzizit: Designed NOT by Women

I've been washing tzitzit now for about fourteen years. I just don't get it. These holy garments need to be hand-washed. I don't even hand wash delicates. If it's not machine washable, I don't own it. One of my sons figured out that if he just wears the same pair all week, he only has one pair to put away. His twin, however, likes a new pair to wear each day, making washing all of them a lesson in patience and knot removal. It seems that if you put tzitzit in the washing machine and/or dryer, the strings get all tangled and frayed rendering them less than kosher. They have invented these little "tzizit-washing bags" that hold your tzitzit secure during a machine wash. They don't work.

This year I was determined (with much encouragement from my husband's "Do NOT machine wash them") to wash them all by hand. This now became a thirty minute weekly project requiring a large sink, beach towel and mop by the time I was through. Lately, I've taken to machine washing a couple of them at a time, hoping they don't fray and then hand drying them. The dryer seems to be the worst culprit of the two machines. I am wondering why someone has not invented snap-on tzitzit, so they can be removed while the garment is washed and dried and then re-attached. One thing I know for sure, if God had transmitted the details of this law straight to women, we would have ensured that the garment was machine washable and able to "tumble dry on low."

My nine-year-old son recently came into my room and with all the seriousness he could muster up said, "Mom, Please don't ever wash my tzitzit again. It makes them not-kosher." He has figured out that washing them ruins them and that I am no June Clever. It was all I could do to stop from bursting out laughing. Seriously? He said, "Why are you laughing? I'm serious." I told him I was laughing because he's so serious and the thought of never washing his tzizit again is so Bohemian, it made me laugh. Washing tzizit sort of falls into the same category as shoes. You just wear them until they are no longer functional, too filthy or too stinky. Tzizit were designed with the same engineering. He's also told me he wants a special pair to sleep in. Combine them with his sleeping kippah and we have ourselves a regular little Hasidic elf on our hands. As much as I stare at him, bewildered where this child came from, I am in awe of his dedication. Looks like I'm going to be washing tzizit by hand for a while...oops, now how did that pair get into the washing machine?

Sometimes I glare into my drawer and want to put on a tank top without a shell (long sleeve shirt) underneath. Sometimes the weather is just plain hot, and I don't feel like donning my spiritual wear. But, what years ago was necessity for my happiness, I now see was often just physical pleasure, not that there's anything wrong with that. In fact, so much of my happiness is derived from physical pleasures, yet I'm in a religion that pushes me past them. There is not anything inherently wrong with physical pleasure, especially if you throw in a dose of gratitude with it, but here is the key: Judaism is about rising ABOVE nature, above the physical. Everything we do takes what is seemingly natural, whether it is eating, intimacy, physical urges or dress, and kicks it up a notch encouraging attention.... to the divine. As Orthodox Jews, we look for the divine within every *waking moment*. Sometimes I just need a good nap.

All in a Day's Rest

"The meaning of the Sabbath is to celebrate time rather than space. Six days a week we live under the tyranny of things of space; on the Sabbath we try to become attuned to holiness in time. It is a day on which we are called upon to share in what is eternal in time, to turn from the results of creation to the mystery of creation; from the world of creation to the creation of the world." Abraham Heschel

Shabbat Shalom! Good Shabbos! These greetings are the anthem for all Jews, religious or not. The Sabbath is central to our existence as Jews, for as the proverbial remark says, "it is not the Jews who have kept the Sabbath, but the Sabbath that has kept the Jews." For observing Jews, the Sabbath becomes such an integral part of our lives that it literally dictates the rest of our week. This break in time is not a physical rest, but
a "holy" day. Shabbos is a rest from creation, from exploration and the mundane. It is a separation, and there is holiness that lies waiting for anyone who wants to pursue true nirvana on the Sabbath day.

I was told that I would acquire a second soul on the Sabbath, and that the pleasure of the Sabbath is only a fraction of the *world to come.* Problem was that I was hardly in tune with my first soul. To acquire this spiritual nirvana one needed to plan, shop, cook and clean before the Sabbath began, and then pray, eat, and often entertain, all while avoiding thirty-nine work prohibitions. These work prohibitions are related to tasks that were assigned to the building of the Mishkan (tablernacle) in the desert, such as, winnowing and threshing, just to name a couple. I was pretty sure I wasn't winnowing or threshing and quite confident that no one around me had been doing such since the 15th century; although, to be honest, I wasn't exactly sure what winnowing or threshing entailed.

But, apparently, I need not fear as there were volumes of books to explain all of this to me. There were even children's books with cartoons pictures to explain things such as winnowing and threshing as well as gathering, sorting, grinding, sifting, kneading, cooking, shearing, dyeing, spinning, warping, weaving, tying, tearing, trapping, flaying, writing, erasing, building, and so on. In addition, the thirty-nine prohibitions had been translated into modern day tasks and were really like three hundred and ninety prohibitions with close to three thousand interpretations, including things like not turning lights on and off or not ripping toilet paper. Did God really care about our ripping toilet paper? Not really sure, but apparently it was important. So although some people owned their own little toilet paper elves (spare family member) and chose to rip ahead, I invested in pre-torn toilet paper, which was something of a cross between a tissue and a paper towel but cost a whole lot more. Ouch. I'd often show up as a guest, donating this toilet paper to the host, who was more than excited to acquire some of the golden paper. In addition, something as simple as making a cup of tea became complicated all in the name of avoiding the transgression of these melachot (tasks). So, whereas "keeping the Sabbath and making it holy" may seem subjective and left up to personal interpretation, for Orthodox Jews, keeping the Sabbath is directly related to an avoidance of specific work or creative tasks.

In addition to the task prohibitions, there is the social aspect of having guests. Some guests plan ahead and some "pop-in." We often host such guests as well as we are the recipients of other's hospitality. When my husband and I first moved into our community there were only a handful of people living within walking distance. We realized right away that if we were to be welcomed (and to get involved) we had better step up and do some inviting. Not only is it a feel-good, Abraham-like (minus the tent, sandals and direct line to the Almighty), great social time to have guests, but also it really creates the Shabbos environment.

Food on the Sabbath had to be prepared properly. Sabbath food cannot be cooked on the Sabbath and yet eating warm food is recommended and so has to be heated according to specific halachic rules. For example, prepared foods that are dry are considered cooked, so, once you read the twelve-page manual, no problem heating them up on a hot plate or blech (metal plate that diverts the heat), although not in an oven or directly on a stove. Yet, foods containing liquids have to be indirectly heated so as not to continue cooking them. Certain utensils cannot be used, and the instructions and rules go on and on. This is all, of course, done in the merit of the holiness of the day, but amidst the details I would sometimes find myself feeling quite unholy, annoyed and stifled. I was going through the motions, and my only intention was a twenty-six hour survival on this Shabbos island. Mordechai would suggest that I learn the origins and basis of the rules, but they were so tedious and boring plus, honestly, I just didn't like being told to learn anything. The rules seemed so devoid of spirituality. Once again, I would soon learn that I was mistaken.

My turning point really came from the women of my community who extended their homes, support and understanding. Eventually I did learn, and I still do continue to learn, sometimes the hard way and sometimes the right way. But, here's the thing. You just can't do this without learning. It's like driving a car without ever reading a rulebook. You're probably not going to have a successful road trip *and* you just can't start out on the highway.

In addition to avoiding the prohibitions, I had to learn to cook things like kishke, cholent and kugel, and not just any kugel. I had to learn to make what my husband called, "the kugel." This was to be "the kugel of all kugels." My mother had a recipe for an amazing sweet kugel, but my husband insisted on the Hasidic kugel. Being that I don't like to cook anything with more than three ingredients, this posed a problem to my husband who was anticipating warm kugel on any given Friday afternoon in preparation for Shabbos. I offered him and my kids those pre-made-home-baked chocolate chip cookies instead. It's not that they didn't love the cookies, but he was pining for his kugel. So, like any man married to a culinary-challenged-wife, he learned to make it himself. Thank God!

THE Kugel

It seems that to have a REAL Shabbos experience in a Hasidic home, one must partake of potato kugel (Jewish potato soufflé). Typically, when one visits a religious home in a traditional Hasidic community, one is immediately, upon entering the home, served piping hot, homemade potato kugel. As my husband reminded me on many occasions of his "kugel experience" upon visiting various places in New York, I couldn't help but imagine June Cleaver in a sheitel (she did wear one didn't she?), welcoming my husband into her home with piping hot kugel in hand. I did not grow up with this particular "religious experience" (we had piping hot apple pie), but I did get the chance to experience it at a religious home where we stayed while visiting relatives (whom did not keep Shabbos and we could not stay with), and, yes, it was delicious. Children suddenly appeared out of the walls (and we did too) when the kugel was presented an hour or so before Shabbos began. There is nothing quite like homemade, piping hot kugel.

Anyway, it seems that persistence pays off. My husband insisted that he just could not go another Shabbos without making THE kugel. I offered to make it for him to which he said, "Oh no. I'm going to make it myself. You have to have the exact recipe." I was happy to step aside knowing that this was more of his OCD (Orthodox control disorder) than any real insult to me. I have been known to "experiment" with recipes (I consider any white substance a substitute for any another) and the kugel recipe was not to be experimented with (commandment number 11: Thou

Shalt Not Alter the Kugel Recipe). My only suggestion was that perhaps instead of putting potatoes through the food processor that my husband purchase already shredded potatoes for his first go at the recipe. He agreed. Kugel number one was a beauty! On a scale of one to ten it visually received a nine and a half. We dug into this masterpiece only to find ourselves gasping for water as the pieces got caught in our throats. The kugel was.....you guessed it...too dry. But, such a shame, as it was a beauty (crispy on the outside, white on the inside). The second week, my husband proceeded to try the kugel again. This time he insisted on using fresh potatoes and the food processor. Well, folks, au natural it was indeed. This kugel was, I don't know how to say it, multicolored: gray, brown and white. On a scale of one to ten it received a two for its appearance. We devotedly dug into this kugel, but it was so slippery that we could have used it to change the oil in our cars. A few kugels later he discovered the "cold potato technique," which keeps the potatoes white. Apparently, if you put your peeled potatoes in ice-cold water and soak for a while, they will stay white. If you put them in the refrigerator they will stay even whiter. White potatoes can turn a horrible looking kugel into what at least looks edible.

To date, we have finally had "the Kugel" (try number ten was the winner). It was soft, white, fluffy and delicious, and as you might guess, lulled us off to sleep as anything with potatoes and oil will do.

So, I was cooking, cleaning, preparing, learning and praying, but I just wasn't getting into the pleasure of the Sabbath. I had not hit nirvana.

I did what anyone would do who is missing out on pleasure. I went online and Googled "pleasure" and found Mama Gena, "the pleasure expert." Mama Gena impressed how important pleasure was to our well-being. Mama Gena suggested that I sit down in a calm, relaxing spot and brainstorm a list (while listening to some soothing music) of all the things that bring me pleasure. I did so. My list had things like taking a walk, playing guitar, petting my dog, riding my bike, hiking and so on. I had about fifteen items or so on my pleasure list. None of them included making cholent or entertaining twenty guests on a regular basis. Apparently, the pleasure of Shabbos and Mama Gena's definition of pleasure were not related.

Anyway, Shabbos in this new community was an experience. I was looking forward to this day of peace, but what I didn't realize was all the work it would take to become so peaceful nor how long these meals would last. First, in order to be a part of the community, we needed to invite guests. This posed an entire new problem. Who would eat at our home? There were people who thought we were too observant and people who thought we were not observant enough. There were people with dietary restrictions, screaming children, and elderly parents (neither of those could sit for too long). There were people who didn't like pets or whose children were terrified of our eight-pound miniature dachshund. We finally decided that our mission would be to invite, provide food and entertain. The entertainment was my husband's gift to our guests, consisting of several divrei Torah (inspiring words of Torah) that were more like a series of mini speeches stretching our meals out to a few hours.

Today our Shabbos meals are truly an experience. In addition to the words of Torah, our seudah (festive meal) consists of singing, discussions and enough food to have you not needing to eat for about twenty-four hours after the meal. One of the dishes that we serve is a thick brown stew that practically cooks itself, while in a crockpot for about twenty-four hours, into an almost inedible matter called Cholent. Cholent contains meat, beans, potatoes and just about anything else you'd like to throw into the pot. It provides the warm food necessary to make the meal festive. It literally puts fat and meat on your bones and turns itself into a thick brown sludge, if left to its own accord. Leftover cholent can be eaten again (for the brave at heart) or used as mortar to lay brick. It is traditional to have cholent on Shabbos day. It is also obligatory to say, "Mmm. This is great cholent (even if you are choking on it)!" People always talk about two foods at the table: the challah (bread eaten on Shabbos and it also gets the obligatory "Mmm" even if it's raw like dough or burnt and hard as a rock) and cholent. There are even cholent contests. Should you attend one, beware. You will need to stay far away from other people for several days afterward. The beans are lethal.

We frequently have guests to our home. Some are regulars, some are the occasional friends that we have over, some are new faces, some are the B&B (bed and breakfast) and some are B&B&D&L&T (bed &breakfast & dinner & lunch & third meal) guests. These are people passing through town who need a "Shabbos stop." You see, when you sign up to be observant, you also sign up to "be like Abraham," (yes the biblical one) and like Sarah (yes, the biblical one), who opened up their tent (on all four sides, no less) with the smell of piping hot challah wafting out to all passer-byers. I'm pretty sure they did not have a tent for twenty. At any rate, we actually enjoy sharing this hospitality and we frequently have guests with whom we share our home and Shabbos meals. I try to warn them. Some take heed and others do not.

Standard Work

A few years into our new Shabbos experience my husband returned from one of his adventures to New Square, New York and requested a more "standard" Shabbos experience. He felt that our meals should be more of a "service" to God and should not be a social hour. Huh? But, I liked the social part! Who would now want to come sit attentively at our table other than our miniature dachshund? You may disagree with this approach, which I did also, but looking back, I will tell you that the change

68

eventually elevated our meals. We also lost a few guests along the way (even the dog got bored), but like all good things, there is sacrifice. And, like all changes that occurred through the years, my husband swung us way to the right, I slammed the brakes on and we ended up just a bit "left" of his "right."

At the time of this change, I was working for a corporation that incorporated a policy called "standard work." It was like halacha for the workplace. It prevented anyone from deviating or getting too creative without permission. I'm not too hip on standard work. I prefer the "un"standard work. My husband told me he wanted to implement standard Shabbos meals, standard songs (sung at the same time) and standard serving of the food. Basically, he wanted to standardize the Shabbos Seudah. This was not to create discomfort but rather to create a standard. For some a standard creates energy, like a marching band or an army. There is a sense of energy gained from the standardization. For others, it can be stifling. I hesitated, but relented, reluctantly dragging my heels, honestly feeling as if another joy had been zapped out of my life.

As my sister in law would often comment, "You must really love that man." Love is a bi-product of any committed marriage. My hesitation with the request was in that I wanted my guests to feel comfortable. Carmelle, sixteen at the time, offered to make me cue cards, as I initially kept botching up the order of things, frustrating my husband to no end. It baffled him that I couldn't remember during which part of the "niggun" (a song without words and a lot of 'la-dee-das') to bring out the food. What he didn't understand was that I was trying to juggle four courses, six to eight platters, hot plates, serving utensils, condiments and dishes...and bring them all out on cue while not traifing (making non-kosher) my kitchen and keeping everyone happy! Seriously?? I honestly envisioned dropping a platter in his lap. One day, I just found myself giggling at it all. I'm not sure which part I found amusing, but I just realized that it just wasn't all that important. I would do my best, and he would have to get over my faux pas. Besides, he cooks a large majority of the food, so I really couldn't complain too much. I even offered letting him serve all the food from his seat at the table.

He declined.

But the truth is, this all came together and I was happy to do it all, for just one thing: a warm, loving look...from his end of the table. Man, what a girl will do for a little attention.

All In a Day's Rest

So, my pleasure list was missing Shabbos, or for that matter, anything ritually Jewish. And, then I realized that the pleasure

70

that is brought forth from Shabbos has nothing to do with all the physical pleasures that would make me "feel good." All the physical pleasures were great for my body and mind, but the pleasure that I was missing out on Shabbos came from my higher self, one that I really didn't know.

Although, I realized that my soul needed a lot of work, to say the least, there were many Shabboses when I also needed a second body. It was my body that was exhausted from shopping, cooking, cleaning, washing dishes, setting tables and moving garbage. Mordechai was a huge help, but there were times I needed a wife! I secretly longed for biblical times where one man had multiple wives, as I really needed a few more hands. Instead, I became Lucille Ball. If you could imagine an episode of the Lucy Show with Lucille Ball trying to make challah, kugel, chicken soup, chicken, salads, fish and dessert, by the time Ricky walked in the door, well, that was me. If I could add a footnote to the Torah it would look like this: "...and on the Seventh day you shall rest" (after you totally exhaust yourself on days five and six preparing for the REST and days three and four shopping to feed a small army of guests.)" I learned quickly that Shabbos required a lot of work.

It sometimes took me two or three evenings of preparing meals and at least half the day on Friday to get ready. I just wondered if this was how it was all supposed to work. It seemed that the week had been put in place to serve the Sabbath, but I wondered if we had it wrong. Maybe the Sabbath had been established to maximize our potential as human beings during the week. Either way, my week was shrinking and I needed a wife.

And then there were my saviors. The phone would ring, and someone would invite us over for a meal.

Yes!

One of our favorite invites is always to our rabbi's home. To get the feel of a Shabbos in our community in Dunwoody, Georgia (Congregation Ariel), one needs to spend several Shabboses with our rabbi and his wife, the infamous Mora Dena, although, just one would serve as a memory. This is not mandatory by any means, but quite an experience, or privilege I must say, not to be missed; and it sets a tone for our community at large. There are simply no words to describe these amazing people. They are filled with love, warmth, inspiration, understanding and well, just a bit of humor too. They have to. Not only do they practically run a soup kitchen for the religious seekers, but they have about twenty electronic wall clocks that go off at every hour, about thirty seconds apart from one another, yes, even on Shabbos. It just wouldn't be the same at the Friedman's without Torah, burnt chicken and the Lucille Ball theme song in the background.

Brown Food Cafe

A Sabbath meal at the Friedmans is usually for no less than forty people. Other than her daughters, who eventually grew up and moved away, there is no kitchen help either. Rebbetzen Friedman (or Mora Dena as she is so fondly known) prepares food while standing up, often until 3:00 a.m., and often with her eyes closed. I refer to her meals as the Brown Food Café (she laughs at that and says I'm too generous as it should really be the "Black Food Cafe"), because she intentionally over-cooks everything until it was well-well-well done and a tan-brown-black color, a bi-product of her not wanting to undercook anything for fear of anyone of her forty+ guests getting sick on her watch. When I first became observant, I thought it was a law that food had to be cooked to a brown color.

In addition, the Friedmans will never turn away a guest. Another few guests? No problem. She'll just chop everything up a bit smaller and set another place at the table. Add the experience of sitting at their table with their twenty-five to forty guests, listening to Rabbi Friedman's warm voice, the brown food (plus her colorful fruit mush!), divrei Torah (words of Torah), singing and just a lot of schmoozing (talking) and laughing and you have an experience like no other. I often look at our rabbi and Rebetzen and wonder if they are happy. But, I don't think happy is something that concerns them. They smile and laugh a lot. But, their happiness is a byproduct of their purpose. And, they never sway from their mission. My favorite part of Shabbos? It is hard to say, but for sure it is either listening to Rabbi Friedman talk or sitting in the Friedman home surrounded by all their guests and the Friedman smiles. I often pine to be a guest at their home. There is just no experience like it. Besides, they keep inviting us. It must be the red pickled beets that I keep bringing over. But I think, it's just, well, where we are... loved.

There are times I now actually feel uplifted by Shabbos, but I've learned that it's not only for me to be uplifted but to do some uplifting. I'm not sure if it's the physical pleasure from slowing down and being electronically *dis*connected, or my soul being in its happy place. On any given Friday night, I am lulled to sleep to the sound of my husband laining(chanting) the Torah portion for the next day. Or, sometimes, I will crawl up in bed or lie in our sunroom facing our lake with a good book. Maybe it is the walk to shul (synagogue) or playing a game with our children that brings me peace. I'm sure it is a culmination of all these things that without the Sabbath, would not occur, but the connection and devotion is still something I am working on. For the real pleasure of the Sabbath comes from being in your "soul space" and that is quite challenging for most of us coming from a focus on the physical. The real pleasure I am told is taking the time to praise God. The Sabbath is our special time to do so.

Shabbos also involves walking, a lot of walking. We walk in nice weather. We walk in rainy, cold weather. We walk in humid, hot weather. We walk short distances, and we walk far. In fact, the upside of Shabbos is the walking. Well, most of the time. There have been times while out of town, we have had to cross major highways or walk in the snow or extreme heat.

Walkabout

A couple weeks ago, my daughter, son and I made a Shabbos walkabout. It's not that it was so far (about two and a half miles each way), it's just that it drew a lot of attention, because it was in ninety-degree heat going and a hundred and six degree heat on our return trip. We received much concern as well as support. We were doing this walk to participate in a celebration for my parents' sixtieth wedding anniversary. The Lord knows I've messed up on quite a few commandments from time to time, so I thought this might be a good way to uphold number four (keeping the Sabbath day) and number five (honoring parents) all at once. You know, a two-for-one deal with the Almighty.

I remember reading a short story about Rabbi Shlomo Carlebach walking thirteen miles to a Shabbaton near LA (1970's) in the cold and rain. It seems Shabbos started before he could get to the synagogue. So, he and his caravan of Jewish Jippies (hippies) got out of the car and walked the rest of the way creating a lot of attention. Other people joined them, even some who weren't Jewish.

I think people, in general, are impressed with commitment. I had a neighbor once remark and marvel at the fact that we walk to our synagogue... no matter the weather: "nice day, cold, snowing or raining...you walk." It's not that our synagogue is such a happening place, although it is full of activity. It is just that the walking creates a commitment, and it's a no-no to drive or ride in a car.

I often wonder how it would affect our natural resources, society and world if everyone took one day a week to walk and put their cars to rest.

Anyway, back to my own Shabbos walk. No one offered to join us...some probably thought we were homeless. We stopped in four gas stations to wet our faces and at my niece's apartment to hydrate, but we made it. We even hid some water bottles in the bushes as only part of the walk was in the eruv (boundary) where it is permitted to carry. It's funny how things like that put the rest of your life in perspective. I even was glad to go sit in the heat for the 4th of July fireworks show, because an eighty+ degrees fireworks evening just doesn't even register compared to a 106 degree walk. I just hope my two-for-one holds out for a while, as I think I may have slipped up on #10: coveting. My neighbor just got two new puppies to offset her divorce. I was secretly wondering if I could trade my husband in for two puppies as well. I'm sure that even thinking this probably cost me a few brownie points.

What I do know is that the Sabbath is a supermarket of spiritual wealth. It is not defined by how we understand space or time. I can only say that its purpose is beyond our understanding, science or nature and yet it's attainable to us at the same time. It is a gift. It is a birth-rite. It is said that it is a taste....of the world to come.

It took me many years, but through the rituals, repetition and learning I have come to relish the Sabbath. There are moments of pure tranquility mixed with singing, joy, laughter, listening, learning, prayer, service, introspection and commitment. And, at the heart of the Sabbath and behind all the rituals lay the foundation of not only the Jewish people, but all people, our entire world and universe.

All Those Holy Days

"Vesamachta beChagecha, ata u'vincha u'vitecha...vehayisa ach sameach" - and you shall rejoice on your festivals - you, your sons, your daughter, etc, and you will be completely joyous (Deutoronomy 16:13).

Most Americans celebrate just a handful of holidays throughout the year. Those holidays usually consist of food, time off of work and shopping, with a large emphasis being on the shopping. Jewish holidays are not exactly vacation days, nor shopping days. We do all the shopping ahead of time and then hoard food away in our homes in preparation for each holiday. Jewish holidays are religious days, with some being more religiously directed than others, depending on their biblical orientation. But, for the most part, they are HOLY days. Each "holy" day commemorates an event, but even more so is a reminder of our holy mission. Some are biblically ordained while others are rabbinic decrees.

Each of these days comes with rituals and mitzvot (requirements). Whereas some holidays are extremely serious, others are quite joyous. There are holidays for every type of person. Do you like to build? Then Succot is your holiday. Got a little pyromaniac on your hands? You can choose Chanukah or Lag B'omer. Do you run a cleaning service or have a bit of OCD? Then Pesach is your holiday. Are you a tree hugger? Tu B'shvat is your holiday. Do you like to dress up in a costume? Then Purim is your holiday. We have a holiday nearly every single month of the year (eleven out of twelve of the months) with some months having more than one. Throw in several fast days throughout the year and you barely have time not to be on holiday. There are times, honestly, when it is hard not to see these days as a bit intrusive. Just when you get into a routine another holiday or restricted period pops up. You simply cannot be an Orthodox Jew and become a creature of habit.

There is no time for getting into a routine. We are constantly readjusting or better yet, recalculating.

The High Holy Days

Every year the high holidays (Rosh Hashanah, Yom Kippur, Succoth, Simchat Torah) would roll around and it would baffle me that I was baffled again. As much as I was trying to climb up spiritually, the number of meals to be prepared in front of me sidetracked me into a slight depression. It's not that I don't enjoy the entertaining, guests, or that my husband doesn't help out, in fact, he's a far better cook than I am. It's just a bit overwhelming at times to think of preparing twenty-three meals over the three-week period. I fantasized hiring a personal shopper and chef. But, then I would listen to a class online or read a book about Teshuva (repentance) and I would be reminded that all of this serves a much higher purpose, even higher than brisket or potato kugel served times twenty-three.

New Squares

It is that time of year again (thank God) where we plan and prepare for the New Year. I'm counting squares, well, counting meals, well counting how many festive meals to serve between Rosh Hashanah and Simchat Torah. It's a few rounds of eat eat, eat, eat-to-prepare-to-starve, starve, eat-after-starving, eat, eat, eat, eat, eat, eat, eat, eat. For many of us (and count yourself lucky if you are able to take this time to focus solely on self improvement) this means preparing twenty-three major festive meals over the three weeks. This is one of those years where the religious days (first two days of Rosh Hashanah, first two days of Sukkot, etc.) bump right up to Shabbos, creating three-3-day religious marathons over the next month. When you add up all the religious days and their meals, it comes out to around twenty-three meals. It is something like trying to get ready for a snowstorm, three times over. So, I have made myself a little chart. There is a square for each meal where I can note who is coming (God help them) and what we will be eating. As my friend Kim says, no one can dial and order food like us. Anyway, I have my little chart showing whom I've invited and what I'll be serving. I've started doing some cooking when my husband announces that the Kabbalah (mystical Judaism) suggests that one should actually have guests on the last Shabbos of the year prior to Rosh Hashanah to bring in the New Year right. Seriously? You're adding to the marathon? To my squares?

I think that is in the same category as praying after the shofar is blown on Yom Kippur (extending the fast). You're just so proud of yourself for making it twenty-six hours without food and water, and there are people who say, "No, there's more praying to do!" You're thinking: "I just made it twenty-six hours without food or water. With all due respect to the Almighty, we'll have to chat later. I'm outta here!" It's not that I was going to skip Shabbos or anything like that! But, I probably would have let it slip by without inviting guests. The Kabbalah card always wins. I mean, you just can't mess with mysticism. You know there are all these quantum physic theories about quarks, and who knows what and I'm just not messing with them..... and I don't mean to complain, but just when I was patting myself on the back for planning ahead, wham! That's the thing with Orthodoxy....there's always more. As my Buby used to say: "You give them a finger and they want your entire elbow."

Anyway, last night I invited my sister for one of the meals. She said, she would be out of town and suggested another day. That was not a day with a square. So I told her, you have to fit into a square. No square, no meal. Surely out of the twenty-three squares, she can find one to fit into? Actually, she is already in one square, but as family, it is her right, her punishment, to be offered a second square. We also try hard to invite people who might otherwise not have a place to go, or "friends" whom we feel need to be spiritually enriched (or tortured) and then throw in some ambiguous people, like "the Russian lady." I'm sure she has a name, but with my not-so-good-memory (and have you ever noticed that Russian names don't remind you of anything?), I have a hard time remembering them.

Well, at least I know I have something to work on this year. So, as I am trying (really hard) to feel connected to God (and remembering Russian names), while chopping salad, finding special foods, and ordering kosher food on line, I want to take this opportunity to wish you all a healthy, happy new year. May you be sealed in the book of life AND one of my little squares! By the way, I picked some awesome friends who will rock the end of my year and catapult me into the New Year in God loving, soul stirring style. Of course, my little dachshund is not complaining, as there will be more good sniffs (and maybe a few extra crumbs) to be had. And, once again, my husband was right, darn! You just can't roll over into the New Year. You have to go into it with style. Rosh Hashanah, here I come!

In addition to the holidays and fast days, every month we celebrate Rosh Chodesh (the new moon). In fact, the observance of the new month was the very first commandment given to the Jewish people and the first holiday we observed as a nation leaving Egypt during biblical times. Rosh Chodesh is particularly special for women as a reward for our not participating in the golden calf fiasco (Exodus:32). Apparently, our avoiding the calf resulted in our receiving moon privileges. Sometimes women will get together on the new moon to learn, bake, pray or have a special program like a bracha party. This is where we eat foods from different food groups in the merit of someone special and everyone in the room says, "amen" to each person's blessing over each food. It's sort of like group therapy... with food, of course.

There is always a focus on food, whether it is food we are required to eat or food we are abstaining from eating. But, don't be misled. There is always thought, gratitude and intention with every bite and bite and bite.

More importantly, the holidays are points throughout the year when we have an opportunity to reconnect directly with ourselves, our purpose, our souls and with God. It was explained to me that a person has an essential, natural, internal need to be joyous at regular intervals - in the same way that he needs food, rest and sleep. God wanted to give us, His people, merit for all our deeds. Therefore, He provided us with festivals, when we commemorate the miracles and favors that He showed us.

Holidays are not about showing up to synagogue, although that helps, or getting a new outfit, although that helps, a lot. When I was first married, I would sit up in the balcony of our synagogue and watch the fashion show parade in front of me. I wasn't exactly focused on the task at hand. Holidays are really not even about the food. I know that's a shocker. The holidays (each one with its own unique purpose) get us back to our roots, tell a story of where we came from and direct us to where we are going. There is no Jewish holiday that exists simply because of tradition. I remember the year my twins were in public school and I was instructed to bring in kosher candy for their gingerbread house (the teacher was very sensitive to our spiritual pallet). I had never made a gingerbread house, so I volunteered to come in and participate. I turned to the lady next to me and asked, "So why do you make gingerbread houses?" She had no idea but said something like, "It's a tradition." I then asked her when we'd be eating them. "Eating them? You don't eat them!" Huh? We were making a house out of food that we could not eat? That tradition would never last in a Jewish community. We would *never* make something out of food that we could not eat.

The historical significance of each holiday is not like a history line. We believe that each year we repeat the lessons, in consecutive cycles, and we hope we keep circling closer and closer to God. In addition, we don't have holidays that celebrate individual people. There is no Moses Day. Jewish holidays signify our mission. Each holiday has meaning and divine purpose tied back to a very specific event that transformed us as Jews.

Heads or Tails

There is a custom on Rosh Hashanah to eat symbolic foods. As with many customs in our home, we take this as a commandment, not a choice. So, each year we consume the traditional symbolic foods (apples and honey, leaks, dates, carrots, beets, etc.) while saying things like "we'll 'beet' our enemies and have a 'sweet' new year and may our pipes not 'leak." We always add in the half a raisin and celery so we may "have a raise in salary." I decided this year to eat two raisins with celery so that I should have a double raise in salary. One year we ate at our friend's house. They did not serve the half a raisin and celery. That year my salary was cut in half. I now travel with my celery and half a raisin, just in case.

Anyway, one of the traditions is to eat a fish head. Yes, you read that right. In fact, some people actually use a sheep's head. This is so that we may be like the "head" and not the "tail." Really smart people buy the little candy fishies and eat the heads off. I have bought a fish head in past years. We have placed it on our table and then placed it in the trash. This year my husband decided (via the suggestion of a seven year old) to go and catch fish from our lake (more like a pond).

So, out he went with our twin boys in tow and the bait (the new fluffy sandwich bread that I had just brought home for sandwiches). He proudly came back an hour later with several brim, placed on ice in zip lock baggies and asked if we wanted to view them. My daughter and I declined.... vehemently. The poor fish went into our freezer to be dealt with later. Five days later he inquired from a local Orthodox fisherman as to how to prepare the fish. The fisherman told him to first throw them out. It seems that unless you gut the fish immediately, they will become septic. My daughter and I were already beginning to see the glory of trusting one's own instincts when it comes to survival skills...or at least to eating things less than desirable.

So, back to the pond went my husband, twins in tow and, yes, more fresh bread. But, this time they brought along the Orthodox fisherman's son, Jake. Jake was more than happy to lend his expertise for the mitzvah and not only showed his skills as a fisherman, but also literally saved one poor fish from escaping by catching it with his bare hands. In addition, Jake gutted our new brim and provided us with gutless brim to be prepared for our festive meal. Ah, the joy of fishing. My daughter was fully convinced that the fish we purchase from the store are not REAL fish, as otherwise she would NEVER eat them.

Well, these little fish, minus their tails, were served. Two brave souls consumed them (note: neither twin who witnessed the massacre participated in the consumption) and, so we had another new year at the head....and not the tail.

Squirrel Be Gone!

We have squirrels. In our attic. In our yard. In our gutters. I've been watching them climb up our electrical wires to our roof, carrying foliage to build their winter *home in my attic. They are busy little creatures. I called up the pest control man, who verified, "Yep, you have squirrels and it will cost you to remove them." It's not that I mind sharing our home, but I just don't like rodents or rodent-looking animals in close proximity. They are cute from a distance.*

The other day, my son comes running in to tell me that there is a dead squirrel in our front yard. He tells me this at 6:30 p.m., Erev Rosh Hashanah. I tell him, "Go tell your Aba (dad) to remove the squirrel." He runs upstairs and comes back. I said, "Well?" He said, "You might want to go talk to him." So, I go up to see what could possibly be holding up my husband from removing the dead squirrel out of our front yard and removing the horrible image from my mind. Surely he doesn't want to leave it there for three more days until the first leg of our marathon holiday is over. We have twenty people coming over for lunch tomorrow, and the squirrel is very noticeable. He tells me, "I have good news and bad news." "Enlighten me," I say. He says, "The good news is that you are going to have a blog to write this week. The bad news is that I cannot remove the squirrel as I just went to the mikvah." I say, "Huh?" He explains that once you use the mikvah, you cannot touch anything dead or it nullifies your "pure state" making the immersion void.

Even using a shovel (of course, how else would one remove a dead animal?), would be like an extension of one's arm and making the "pure state" void. Great! Well, I don't exactly want to contaminate my pure self either at this point. So, I look across the street at my non-Jewish, hard working, lawn keeping, rake-in-the-hand neighbors for a little help. How about I try this on them: "You see, we have a dead squirrel in our yard, and we are too pure to move it right before the Jewish New Year, so do you think you could bring your not-so-pure self over to our yard and remove it for us?" Nah, that probably would not

84

have worked too well and may have limited all the smiles and waves I normally get.

It seems I live across the street from Annie Oakley. That comes in handy at the perfect moment. So, I approach our neighbor and say, "It seems I'm a bit squeamish around dead animals. Do you think your husband could remove our dead squirrel from our front yard? "Oh, Rick? Well, he's not going to do that, but I will." Now, it would have been nice if she thought that my husband was simply not home. But, it doesn't work out that way. She scoops up Mr. Nutty at just the moment that my husband is pulling out to go to synagogue. I open my mouth to explain, and then think... perhaps better to let our neighbors think my husband is a bit eccentric. This one event surely would not be the only cause for those thoughts. I'm sure it ranks right up there with the "hut in their backyard" and "bringing over their beta fish during Pesach because it's food was not kosher." Because, explaining that he is too pure, would just not go over well and would ruin our reputations of being just plain weird.

The most serious holy day is Yom Kippur. Now, truth be told, this biblically commanded fast day, ordained from God, is a gift to us, and it is the time of year when we can truly return to whom we are intended to be. We can realize where we fell short, admit it and then regroup, sort of speak. Now, don't think that we are not guilt ridden each and every day, several times a day. We practically wake up from bed and beat our chests asking for forgiveness, but Yom Kippur stands alone for total and complete atonement. I'm also told that when the Mashiach (messiah) comes, it will truly be a joyous holiday. Until then, it's not. It's very serious. We get so enticed with all the apples and honey from Rosh Hashanah and them bam! It's Yom Kippur. By the time the holiday arrives, it's almost too late. The rabbi always tells us about those who will get life or those who will get death. And just as you've taken your last swallow of water, and you're thinking, "Oh no!" I really shouldn't have sent that horrible email or fed those people the lettuce when I forgot to check for bugs, around comes your Kol Nidre pledge card to assuage you of your guilt.

Yom Kippur

So...this is the time of year when we are soul searching while trying not to think about the food we will not be eating. I just recently saw a show "I Shouldn't Be Alive' where a family went eight days without food. Surely, we can handle one? Our problem is the focus on the food when our focus is NOT supposed to be on food. But, you see that is hard when it is ingrained in us to think about food. I mean, there is always a reason to have food: birth, bar mitzvah, birthday, graduation, Shabbos meal, holiday, wedding, even (for the mourners) at a Shiva (mourning) house. Praying makes me really hungry. Praying all day makes me super hungry. I am generally hungry by the time I get home from Kol Nidre (the evening service).

I have never felt a kinship with Yom Kippur, the Day of Atonement. My husband LOVES it. It is his favorite holiday. Go figure. That just makes me scratch my head. Yes, one does wonder. For many, this is the day when people with really bad-breath, body odor (try coming around an Orthodox shul on the afternoon of Yom Kippur) no make-up and bedroom shoes pray together. We're supposed to forget about our bodies and focus on our souls. I find that challenging given the smelly clientele and my rumbling stomach. He loves the intensity of the day, the devotion and the idea that finally Jews all over the world are experiencing the same thing as he is.

The whole beating the chest and feeling horrible (while I'm really hungry and thirsty) and standing up for long periods of time doesn't do much for me. And, repeating it over and over again doesn't help much. When I was little, my sister and I would play the "Prayer Book

Number Game" to keep busy. One of us would open our prayer book to a page. Then the other one had to try and let their book fall open to the same page. Or, we would do the "Find Your Elbow Game." You close your eyes and someone tickles your forearm. You have to tell them when they get to the crack in your elbow. Apparently, no one wants to play the "Prayer Book Number Game" or "Find Your Elbow Game" with me. Maybe I should offer "Hair or Sheitel Game." It might go over better with my new crowd.

Despite my food longings, I do like where I am at the culmination of Rosh Hashanah and Yom Kippur. It's an accomplishment and ....a gift. A gift to purge and start a new fresh year. The idea that I can survive twenty-six hours without food or water seems to most of my non-Jewish friends nothing short of heroic. And, I love eating when it's over. There are times during the day when I fantasize about food. Oh now, don't be so holy. You do too. But truthfully, those of us who "survive" Yom Kippur cannot really enjoy it. The real joy comes from "thriving" through Yom Kippur.

This year to prepare Yom Kippur my husband tells me that he is holding by Pas Yisroel" (another level of stringency where we only eat grain products baked under Jewish supervision) during the "Aseret Yemei Teshuva (Ten Days of Repentance between Rosh Hashanah and Yom Kippur)." I said, "Oh, this is new?" He says, "No, I've been doing this for ten years." I said, "Huh?" (yes, again). How is it possible that a ten-year tradition has just passed right by me without my noticing? I take full responsibility for being an OCD (Orthodox Compulsive Disorder) enabler. My hubby takes full responsibility for "raising the bar." We are a perfect match.

Anyway, during the ten days it is customary (as I just found out) to up the obsessive food restrictions to "Pas

Yisroel." Okay, well, it seems that unless you live in Brooklyn that is not so simple. Can you imagine that there are people who are Pas Yisroel, Cholov Yisroel, and OCD Yisroel? I typically try to avoid sugary foods during the ten days before Yom Kippur so as to make my fast a bit easier (in addition to hydrating and eating my t-spoon of peanut butter right before the fast....little known secret). So, now without much sugar and being Pas Yisroel for ten days, I'm just plain HUNGRY!

My daughter asked me why this custom came about and whom do we think we are fooling if we go right back to our Non-Jewish, baked bagels after Yom Kippur? Smart girl. So, I told her (in my humble opinion) that it is like showing up at a parent's birthday party dressed the way they like you dressed even if you normally dress differently. It ups the level of respect. So, before we throw a party for God, we dress ourselves up a bit. Well, we will see how this all goes. Either way, I'm up for the challenge as much as I'm yearning for a REAL bagel and a cookie.

As long as we were on topic, she and I were also discussing Teshuva (aka: repentance) the other day. She was wondering if everything is meant to be, then why should we be sorry? It is a great question. We are who we are because of our past, both the positive and the negative. This is how Jewish people have repented for years, and, well it seems, how God intended it (at least the no eating part on the 10th day of Tishrei, as it is commanded). So, I told my daughter that I had a different take on Teshuva (and yes I'm well aware of the three steps: recognize, remorse, repent). Teshuva is a "return." It is, at its most meaningful aspect, a going back to your "soul space," and that is exactly what the word means, "to return." Yet, it's hard to return if you don't acknowledge that you're not there. So, thus the remorse, beating of the chest, etc.

The soul....it is void of fear, angst or anger. It is peaceful. It does not react or need attention. It's not physically needy. It does not care about what others think of it. It is giving in its purest form. It is at one with God. It is a culmination of our choices done from a place of peace, integrity, honesty, oneness.....love. Yom Kippur is a time to get to know your soul once again.

If our bodies are sensory beings (seeing, hearing, feeling, touching, tasting, smelling, thinking, etc.) then our soul is not any of those things. Hmmm...Chew on that for a while...well after you fast. Well, wishing you all an easy fast, a meaningful fast and a good finish. May you be SEALED for life!

After we acknowledge God as "THE King," and return to our rightful soul space, we can finally sit down and party.... with God: outside in a hut, or as we like to call it a "sukkah." This is one of my favorite holidays. As a child, I felt a special connection to this holiday. Our sukkah hung right outside our home on two hooks and a post like a bamboo shower curtain, and we would dress up in our CPO jackets (Chief Petty Officer heavy navy jackets) to stay warm. My mother made the most delicious kiftayas (Sephardic hamburgers) with rice, and we all ate outside. My father covered our sukkah with bamboo and hung up little fruits. I loved seeing the stars through the schach (roof). As much as my mother directed most holidays, this one was where I really saw my parents working together. In our early years of marriage, after our return from Israel, this holiday was where my husband and I began building our own Jewish life together. There is special power in a sukkah... and maybe a few raindrops too. This past year my husband and another crazy yid sat in the rain in the sukkah. That is absolutely not necessary, and after all these years I've learned to consider the source. Anyway, there are a plethora of sukkah laws all located in your handy dandy Gemara, if you read Aramaic. If not, consult your local Orthodox rabbi. But, don't pass this holiday up. Remember that camping trip you promised the kids? Look no further than your backyard sukkah. It's the perfect holiday for the boy or girl scout in you. Not a boy scout? No problem. Just Google "sukkah" and one can be shipped right to your front door that you can pop up in minutes.

Holiday in the Hut

I "survived" Yom Kippur and actually did a little "thriving" too. So, after fasting we "break" our fast at my sister's house. This is an annual tradition. We had our break-fast amongst a very diverse crowd of people, many of whom did not fast. For them it was a "dinner of honor" for those of us who fasted. My sister always makes it a nice occasion for everyone. We make it a point (well my husband is the appointed interrogator) to inquire about the various foods, their whereabouts, from where they came, how they were cooked, who made them, etc., to ensure we don't have to return to shul to beat our chests again (not that that would be the only reason we needed to repent less than an hour after Yom Kippur). Each year my sister takes one more step toward accommodating our religious idiosyncrasies.

So, now we are on to Sukkot (the holiday in the hut). There are VERY specific laws (one would expect no less) regarding the sukkah (how many walls, what the roof can be made of, etc.). Our hut happens to be a full flight of stairs DOWN (and one must come back up at some point) in our backyard. This means about 100 trips up and down the stairs (carrying food, plates, tables, chairs, etc.)making the "stair master" seem like a walk in the park. But, you see, this is THE ONLY SPOT with clear sky on our property, unless we want to put our sukkah at the bottom of our driveway (which will send the homeowners association at us before we eat our first meal). It is imperative that one does NOT place their sukkah under a tree branch. Although my husband tells me I'm wrong, I like to think that in addition to the host of reasons listed in the Gemara, the rabbis didn't think it wise to sit under a falling branch. My dog loves this holiday as she can run in and out of the sukkah finding food scraps in between hunting for chipmunks. She is happy that we have finally figured out where we are supposed to eat.

This week we will finish building our sukkah and decorating it. Each year our walls get filled with posters, pictures that our children have made, hanging fruit and, yes, more and more rabbis. I have finally managed to get one section for family photos. Each year, I sneak in a few more. If I get to the succah wall before my husband, I get first dibs on the best spot. If not, the rabbis get priority hanging.

We are planning to have many guests. For one dinner, we have invited our friends who own a catering service. I mean, what was I thinking trying to cook for a caterer? I do make a killer soup (which I managed to pour over my hand last year....by the way aloe really works) and chocolate chip cookies, which his son LOVES, so chances are we will be in good shape. We will sing and talk until midnight. Our neighbor will wonder why the "crazy people next door" have moved their dinner table outside into a hut covered with bamboo. You see, he doesn't realize that we are dining with God... and a few bugs, mosquitoes and other insects we will get to know much better. He doesn't know that Sukkot is an intense time of joy. So, we sit in the sukkah whether it is cold or hot, rainy or clear. We celebrate, sing and eat. My husband will try to sleep in the sukkah. That will last about an hour. At the end of the week, we will pack this all up and go inside to our "regular" home, and, truth be told, we will miss the sukkah.

We're Not Greek

As a child, I loved the holidays. They were easy: get off school, get a new outfit, show up and eat some great food. One of my favorite holidays (I have a few of those) was Chanukah. Okay, so maybe it had something to do with the presents, but, truthfully, I just loved the songs, the story, the smells, the food and the lights. Chanukah is heroic. It is the story of the small Jewish army (2nd century BCE) defending themselves against the mighty Greeks and winning against all odds! It is a story of miracles where the last pure jug of oil (enough for one day) burned for eight days. The holiday of Chanukah was established after the Torah and so has fewer rules, since God didn't ordain any...so I thought.

But, turn anything over to the rabbis and you get RULES. Turn anything over to Hasidic Jews and you get a lot more praying and singing. Every year we make sure to have one night shared with our extended family. We light the candles and sing the blessings and Maoz Tzur (traditional Chanukah song). As the years went on, I had to warn them, "Uh, we've "added" a few things." They are good sports. Chanukah has divine intervention, and, so as to recognize that, it is celebrated with a set of rituals that when done properly can elevate the festival of lights. Most importantly, we're told over and over again, that we are different. We're not Greek. And, today we're not supposed to identify with being American either. Swallow that. Gulp. That's a tough one. Chanukah is about that exact struggle. We celebrate the struggle, the difference and the victory.

Chanukah Lights

Chanukah is here! As a child, my mother would play Chanukah music in the house, make latkes and pick one night to shower us with gifts. But, I loved all the nights. I never thought there was anything missing, anything else to be had. I pitied my non-Jewish friends, who in my opinion, were really missing out. I enjoyed seeing their trees and lights, but in no way did it compare in my mind to the joy of Chanukah. I loved the smells, the sounds, the taste and the sights of this miraculous holiday.

As an adult, I have come to appreciate all of my childhood memories as well as the deeper significance of this holiday. The miracle of the oil, the hand of God in every aspect of the story, the significance of the oil, the Macabees, the tiny army winning against the Greeks and the twenty-fifth day of Kislev are all just, well, MIRACULOUS. And miracles we know are just awesome acts of nature, that is, unexplainable events that happen at EXACTLY the perfect moment...the hand of God.

As an Orthodox Jew, I have also come to appreciate this holiday, as it appeared to be a reprieve from the many rules that all the other holidays have....So I thought. Yet, if there is a place to add a ritual, my husband will put one in. So, I'm sitting in a class this week learning about Chanukah, when our class leader explains that after lighting the candles, you can go right into singing Maoz Tzur. I say, "Well, not if you're in our home." The entire class looks at me. "You do more?" they ask. "Oh yes," I explain that my husband adds in "stuff." At this point in my life, I will take whatever "stuff" he wants to add, as I won't turn away anything that might bring more Godliness, sparks and blessings to our home. The leader then continues to explain that there was a time when you had to put your menorah out on a porch, but that no longer applies. I say, "not in our house." Once again, the class looks my way. They say, "What is going on in your house?" I tell them, "You have no idea." This past year when my extended family came over to celebrate Chanukah, I had to prep them. "There's just a few more prayers than you are traditionally use to," I told them. My sister didn't mind, as long as we were singing. Anyway, the class decided they were all going to drive by to see our gargantuan oil burning menorah out on our front porch. This pleased my husband to no end.

THEY'RE "CHANUKA BALL" EARRINGS, SILLY... WHAT **ELSE** COULD THEY BE?

Last year, a friend of mine at work let me choose a set of her homemade "holiday" earrings. I naturally picked out the blue ones as they reminded me of Chanukah. Since it was already past Chanukah, I tucked them away to be worn the next year. So today, I donned my Chanukah earrings. As I entered my husband's office he looked at me (somewhat shocked and somewhat bemused) and said, "Have you lost your mind? You are wearing Christmas tree ornaments in your ears!" Truthfully, this never crossed my mind. I was living in my little blue ball bubble.

I said, "No. They are Chanukah balls." He looked at me (like you might look at someone who has really lost their mind), and said, "Ilana... There is no such thing as 'Chanukah balls.'" This had my older son bent over laughing, wondering how he ended up with these parents.

I am still happily wearing my Chanukah balls. My husband is still scratching his head, wondering how after twenty-three years of marriage, I can still shock him. I think maybe I should hold off on the blue stockings for a while.

So this year, we will proclaim the miracle of Chanukah with (God willing) our entire family around us. We will fill our home with the wonderful smell of potatoes, onions and oil (it really proclaims the miracle, as our neighbors can smell it up and down the street). We will shower our kids with gelt and gifts, and then I will sit and watch our oil and candles burn (a small commandment that I can live with). I will think about Yehudit, the Chanukah heroine, who knew when it was time to take things into her own hands. She depended on no one but herself (and God) as she decapitated the Greek commander. At the heart of every great Jewish holiday is at least one great woman. May this holiday bring many blessings to all women, their husbands, their children and families and especially to my mother, who taught me to love Chanukah.

Happy New Year...for the Trees

Tucked in the middle of the winter, just when things seem bleak, cold and lifeless, is Tu B'shvat, the holiday for trees. I love this holiday. My husband actually thinks I was an Indian in my past life. I am very comfortable in a forest amongst the trees. I am consistently dragging him and my boys to go hiking, camping and even RVing, as humorous as that may be. On our last camping trip, I insisted on cooking spaghetti in the woods and bringing our little dog, Cloe. One hour after we arrived, Cloe was standing by the car ready to go home. Two hours after we arrived my husband left, happily, to go to work (and take a shower for his night shift at the hospital). At 10:30 p.m.

my boys and I packed up our tent and headed home. The heat and humidity won. My dog was ecstatic. Even so, I love the woods. We actually have four different new years throughout the Jewish calendar, and Tu B'shvat is the new year for the trees. It usually falls sometime in February, when the trees are about to bud. My name, Ilana, means tree, so I feel a particular connection with this holiday which focuses on thanking God for all that He provides us...from the trees. My husband likes to have a Tu' B'shvat Seder every year. It's not too long and there are fun foods to nibble and taste. We invite friends to join us. We have one set of friends who sometimes forget when we've invited them, but we keep inviting them anyway. They have character and like the rest of us always have a story to tell. Anyway, we love their company and often invite them for our Seders. One year we had just about given up on their attendance when they showed up at the door....with a peach tree. I was so thrilled...at both their arrival and the little tree. We promptly planted it in our backyard. Hopefully the people living here in about thirty years will see fruit.

Tu B'shvat Another Seder?

Today is Tu'Bshevat, The Jewish birthday for trees. I happen to really like this tree-hugging holiday as 1) my name means tree and 2) there are no rules...and I could do with fewer rules. So, last night we invited a few friends and family over for our annual Tu B'shevat Seder. My son asked me why we weren't going over anyone else's house for this annual event. I explained to him that no one else in our community has a Tu B'shevat Seder. He said, "So, why do we live here? Why are we the only ones doing this?" He had that "you grown-ups are so messed up" look.

Tu B'shvat is not just a "tree holiday." We do not worship trees or decorate them. Tu B'shevat is a time in the middle of the winter when everything begins to revive from being dormant. There is no active life, and yet the potential is so great. The sap is moving within the tree and soon the trees will begin budding. So, we take this time to celebrate what will be. We have a Seder (festive "orderly" meal, of course) complete with four cups of wine. We present four "worlds" of fruits from the first world being very physical (the first platter has fruits with a hard outer shell, like nuts, representing the bad parts of ourselves that we wish to overcome) to the last being very spiritual (the last platter has no shells or seeds and is fragrant representing our purest spiritual selves). So, too, we move from the physical, closer to our source, and to being more spiritual. We had our "no -rules" spiritual fruit-lift. And, we even have healthy snacks to munch on for a few more days!

When spring rolls around our holidays begin to pick up again. A really joyous holiday and a favorite for any party-goer is Purim. Kids (of all ages) love Purim as we get to dress up and eat loads of candy. Purim is our reminder of the story of Esther and how she triumphed over the horrible Haman. There are certain commandments for this holiday such as attending a Purim seudah (festive party). I mean how hard can that be? We also give gifts to the poor, listen to the story being read from a scroll and give two food items (misloach manot) to a friend.

Jewish people don't really understand the concept of a small number like two, so we make baskets full of items and deliver them to no less than twenty-five plus friends. Some people avoid this by sending you a card that says a donation was made in your honor in lieu of gifts. Basically, you didn't make the cut. We go driving around our neighborhood delivering little food baskets that our friends don't really want, but it's fun and our kids love hopping in and out of the car and depositing food. Every year we make a list and then as we're driving around we inevitably run into someone we either left off our list or who didn't exactly make it onto the list. We then quickly recycle an already received bag being sure to keep the things we really want to eat. One year we kept passing the same car. The people inside were also delivering food baskets but they were not on our list. Oops. We tried to act inconspicuous, hoping they might not notice us or that they would, God forbid, try to hand us a food package when we didn't have one for them. At an impulse my husband says, "Duck! So they don't see us!" Not so easy while driving.

Then, there was the year we passed another car several times while delivering. Finally, we both awkwardly unrolled our windows to say "Happy Purim." They were not on our list and I'm guessing we weren't on theirs either. I murmured to my husband, "Quick, give them a gift." My husband froze. Those few seconds felt like twenty minutes. And, then there are those people who never leave their homes. When you show up, they hand you a gift. One year, while dropping off a food gift to one of the rabbis in our community, his wife sent their son out to deliver a gift to us while we waited in our car. He didn't feel like walking the entire ten feet to our car so he catapulted the bag filled with a soda and crackers toward my open van window. I caught it in mid air, just as it went crashing into the side of our van. Delivery accomplished. It is a Purim memory not to be forgotten.

I relish the holidays and have not only come to appreciate but love what my husband has brought to our home and our lives. Amongst the chaos and food preparation, I can take a moment to appreciate the significance. Of course, there have been some less than stellar moments. Every year I gawk over all the Pesach vacation brochures and contemplate running away only to find my rational-self keeping me put. One year during Pesach preparations I was feeling overwhelmed (yes, a recurring theme). I simply could not take one more rule, obsession or requirement, or I thought I'd explode. Well, Mordechai didn't listen to me, and he added one more "request." He said, "I don't know what you're so upset about. I just need you to...." I picked up a five-pound bag of sugar and threw it at him. It felt great....for about five seconds. It exploded all over our recently cleaned kitchen. I am not so proud of that moment where I lost all control, but at the time, I had only regret: that it hadn't been a bag of *flour*. I now keep a backup bag on my shelf for emergency re-education, and Mordechai now takes care of most of the details.

The Exodus

Pesach...Food Obsession Gone Bad

If there was ever a holiday that has evolved into an obsession, Pesach is it! This is the highlight of the year for any individual with an obsessive-compulsive disorder. After cleaning through every nook and cranny in your house, you can obsess over your car, your work place, your garage, your backyard, your purse, your clothing and your underwear drawer. Even poor little Cloe gets her doggie food removed for a chametz-free (leaven-free) brand. And if you're gluten intolerant, this is your holiday for grocery shopping: no wheat, oat, barley, spelt or rye.

Really smart Jews just head for the hills (or exclusive beach resorts) leaving behind all their egos and overinflated packages of food. They are the ones who "really enjoy this holiday." Seriously, take a poll. Those who give Pesach the highest rankings are the ones who skip town.

Nevertheless, I might actually be in the minority. I really like Pesach, and I don't skip town. Yes, it comes with its complications, a few meltdowns, marital disputes and really overpriced food, but there is something very REAL about this holiday. Maybe, it seems so real because we are reminded of the Exodus from Egypt three times daily. Or, maybe it's the fact that we wouldn't be here if it weren't for the Exodus. I mean, I can't even get a family of six from point A to point B in a reasonable amount of time, and, yet, three million Jews somehow managed to all exit

Egypt so quickly that they didn't have time to let their bread rise. That in of itself is miraculous.

Maybe I love the fact that, once a year, I have an excuse to purge my house. I actually like the fact that I can hear the exodus story once again and personally connect. I just wonder how awesome that really was. Would I have had the courage to leave? I hope so. Would I have whined and complained? Most definitely, yes. I hope I would have grabbed my tambourine (or tap shoes) to celebrate the freedom that I had never known before. I'm sure, though, if the Exodus were happening today, there would be a hundred differing opinions as to how, when and where you could shake your tambourine.

This is a pretty awesome time to be Jewish. It's a great time to realize that being free is not about choosing what to wear or what movie to see, but it is an awakening of who you really are. Unfortunately, some of us are still in a mental exile; and as much as we say each year "may we be next year in Jerusalem," I'm not sure we are ready. It's a scary thought to the average American Jew. Either way, Pesach teaches humility, courage, faith and commitment. Happy Pesach and may we really be next year in Jerusalem!

When Can You Eat Your Matzah Ball?

It's a few days before Pesach and to my credit we are rolling smoothly into the holiday. I've cleaned just about everything possible in and outside of my house including my dog's ears (she needs to be highly attentive during the telling of the exodus story which lands her some chicken soup). Anyway, my husband (as of last year) took on another stringency to not eat altered grain products (such as matzah combined with water). It has a fancy name, and a good reason, but, basically, it means no matzah balls...or so I thought. To show this is only a stringency, Hasidim (those not living in Israel) eat matzah balls on the eighth night (In Israel the holiday is only seven days whereas outside of Israel it is eight days).

It seems that actually there is a loophole, so you can eat cooked matzah, if the cooking is done prior to the holiday but after having koshered your kitchen. So, you can un-do the stringency (sort of like a double negative becoming a positive). I get that he gets this. You know how Oprah has those "Ah ha" moments. Well I tend to have a lot of "uh... huh" moments. Which leads me to the question that I have most recently posed to my family (and when not getting an adequate answer) and then to our rabbi: Why did God take us out of Egypt? I'm sure you have your own answer to this, and for some of you it might seem quite evident; but my question really asks, "What was His intention with us?" It wasn't exactly a walk in the park after we left (oh gee thanks for the freedom, now can I please have some water?), and then we were pretty much coerced into accepting a whole buku of rules, dehydration, battles, wandering in the desert, ya da ya da.

The answer is quite lengthy (albeit a very excellent response from my rabbi), but my take away was that good relationships (the real ones) require hard work and commitment. We all want someone to know that we exist, because that makes our relationships real. God perhaps wants the same: for the world to know He exists. And, as our rabbi put it, we are His sales reps. So, back to my husband and his eating (dis)order. Somehow where and when he prepares and eats his matzah balls matters. It is a far stretch and one that I can't exactly intellectualize or relate to, but you have to respect it. The commitment is there and really we are all here for one reason: to build the relationship.

Seders Because we Can...

Last night we celebrated Pesach Sheni (because we didn't get enough mitzvah at the first or second Pesach seders) in remembrance of the Jews who missed the first Seder for reasons of impurity. Of course, I had to ask. "I understand why Pesach Sheni was celebrated for those who missed it, but we didn't miss it. Why are we celebrating it?" Note, these questions, are more rhetorical. Of course, I knew, that we were celebrating it simply, because we can.

...and the Receiving of the Torah

It is 3:00 a.m., Shavuous night (or rather morning), and I am one of many people in attendance at a class in our shul. The one I am attending is titled *The Laws of Preparing Foods for the Sabbath.* There are other classes going on as well. The rabbi teaching us has brought kitchen appliances as props to keep us alert. We need them. One lady is sleeping sitting up. I give her five minutes before her head hits the table. Our daughter and her friend once attempted the All Night Shavuous Learning. They brought their sleeping bags "just in case." Within fifteen minutes they were both asleep on the floor in the coat closet. The all night learning is not mandatory, but highly suggested. But, don't feel guilty if you sleep through another "most" important night in Jewish history. It's just the receiving of the Ten Commandments. No biggie.

Exactly fifty days after we, the Jewish people, left Egypt, we received the Ten Commandments and the Torah. Now, during the seven weeks, between Pesach and Shavuos, we are commanded in the Torah to count the Omer. I don't really know much about the Omer except to count it and that it's another one of those times that interferes with my haircutting schedule. Every time I start to get into a haircut schedule, it gets altered by weeks of no haircuts. God said, "count the omer," and we say, "don't cut your hair." It's like the rabbi's didn't want us to be too clean or too happy for too long. If you ask, you get a combination answer about harvest and spirituality, but nonetheless, we count because God told us to count it. I'm probably not alone in that I don't know exactly what I'm counting, but I get the idea, so I count. We all count. We're supposed to be going up in spirituality during the forty-nine days (seven weeks) of counting. We start counting from the Exodus, which we relive at Pesach. The culmination of this experience is the holiday of Shavuos, the receiving of the Torah. But in truth, it's just the beginning of a six-month communion with God that ends after the high holidays. Shavuos, one would think, would be a world-renowned holiday or at least a major Jewish holiday, but funny enough it's hardly celebrated by anyone other than Observant Jews.

There aren't even too many rules concerning this holiday. There's a lot of talk about flowers, and every year the local Orthodox high school girls approach innocent carpool moms asking us to purchase their wilting flowers for double their value. And, of course, we do. It seems as if the little mountain, which Moses ascended and from which God gave us the Ten Commandments, burst into flowers, so this presents itself as a business opportunity to any Jewish day school. In addition, we typically eat dairy foods, as prior to this time we did not have the laws of meat and milk separation.

So, to remember our receiving these rules, we specifically eat dairy, way too much dairy. If you like cheesecake, you are in luck. If you are lactose intolerant, you are out of luck. Of course, this dairy eating tradition is in conflict to those who believe you should eat meat at any festive meal. They fix that by eating dairy, swishing and swallowing and then eating meat. And, then there is the all night learning. Apparently three million Jewish people, while waiting at the edge of Har Sinai, managed to almost sleep through the receiving of the Ten Commandments. Seems like someone hit the snooze button.

Whoops. So to make up for their faux pas, we now stay up all night learning. Our shul provides us with treats and enough caffeine to give everyone cardiac arrhythmias.

After Shavuos, we have a month to get back into our "normal" routine and then, the Torah tells us, we messed up again. Seems like someone decided to party with a golden calf. We've been paying for that ever since. All I know is it interferes with my hair cuts, yet again. It's three weeks where we cannot get a haircut, listen to music or wash our clothes (for the last nine days). With all the restricted days and fast days mixed in with happy days and celebration, I forget whether I'm supposed to be happy or sad. It's kind of like the clap-on, clap-off light switch they used to sell on TV, except it's happy-on, happy-off. The happy-off days of the summer are called "the Nine Days" and restrict swimming as well as other things. Swimming is considered dangerous and we are to avoid dangerous activities during this time. Apparently none of the rabbis drove with my husband.

Summer Holidaze

The Nine Days of Dirty Laundry

Tonight we enter into a period referred to as "the nine days." This is a period of time leading up to Tisha B'av (the ninth day of Av). The Jewish Community Center is having a concert tonight. I would have loved to attend, had it been on another night. The Israeli Scouts are performing, and they are one of my summer highlights. But, tonight I will forgo the experience for one that is more solemn. Historically, this has been a tragic day for the Jewish people, as both temples were destroyed on this same day (over one million Jews perished during the destruction of the second temple alone), the Spanish Inquisition began, and the spies (Numbers:13) came back with negative reports regarding the land of Israel (all on the ninth of Av). And, as it would be expected, we commemorate these events with self-sacrifice, limitations and you guessed it...a fast day. During the nine days, there are additional prohibitions. It is no coincidence that the prohibition against swimming, for example, occurs mid-summer during the hottest days of the year. Had the nine days been in the winter, we'd for sure been prohibited from wearing coats. In addition, we don't listen to live music, attend parties, throw weddings, or wear freshly laundered or new clothing.

This means that Jewish people who observe the nine days are doing their laundry on the day before. Which means that everyone has drawers full of freshly laundered clothing at the start of the nine days. Thus, another problem occurs. Now that we are not doing laundry, but have just laundered our clothes, how do we not wear freshly laundered clothing? So the solutions I was given were: 1) try your clothes on before wearing them or 2) step on your freshly laundered clothes. Now this makes for an interesting ritual.

So, today I finished the household laundry (minus my daughter's clothing, as she prefers to do her laundry once a month causing our washing machine to literally shake its way out of the laundry room). And, I have left my warm, freshly-laundered clothes in a heap on the floor where my dog has found it a comfortable spot to nap. I suppose that will make it fit to be worn during the nine days.

One other custom during the evening before Tisha B'av is to eat a "seudat hamafseket " (a pre mourning meal). This meal is to consist of bread, hard-boiled eggs and ashes.

"What??" Now, my husband claims that I have a selective memory and that I choose not to remember *certain things. I have to agree that if I were going to choose something to forget, eating an egg dipped in ashes would surely be one of them. Yet, this time I claim that this is a "new" ritual and not something I have ever experienced (I lost count of the new ones a few years ago). Our daughter says, "I'm not eating that. It's not healthy (spoken from a true guardian of health). I ask my husband, "Don't ashes have carcinogens in them?" He does not reply. Looks like we will be eating ashes tonight in preparation to fast and mourn. My friend, Tobi, has always suggested eating a tablespoon of peanut butter before a fast. She claims this is a true hunger-preventer. I am wondering how ash flavored peanut butter is going to feel in my throat. Either way, we will go into Tisha B'av with intention. We will think back to the times of destruction and look to a time when we can rebuild. If you have never had an opportunity to experience Tisha B'av with a community, I suggest you do so. It is meaningful, grounding and a thought provoking experience (with or without the ash-dipped egg).*

May the nine days help us to commemorate those who perished and all that was lost. May the Temple speedily be rebuilt in our days (Amen!); and may everyone be wearing freshly laundered, but slightly dirty, clothing and not smell like ashes.

I grew up, like many American Jews, celebrating both American and Jewish holidays. When I was a teen, I was introduced to the proverbial question: Are you an American Jew or a Jewish American? As a teen, I really identified more as an American Jew. I knew I was different from the other kids on my gymnastics team or people at the 4th of July Fireworks show. It was only as I became more observant that I sometimes wondered if I wasn't living more as a Jewish American. I love this country yet often feel torn between priorities. You may wonder why. The truth is there are times they conflict. It's hard to celebrate the 4th of July on a Shabbos or focus on Chanukah surrounded by all the Christmas media. But, I wear both identities proudly (and truthfully sometimes not so proudly) depending on what either group is doing. At any rate, secular American holidays are a part of our culture, and I believe they define us as much as Yiddish defined our ancestors who lived in Eastern Europe. Mordechai enjoys the American holidays too, but for him there is clear and significant difference.

The Jewish Love Fest...Tu B'Av

Every year when Valentines' Day rolls around, I remember back to my days as a young girl. My father would come home with a small box of chocolates for each of his "girls." He'd hand us the box of chocolates, give us a kiss and say, "Happy Valentines Day." When I got married, I looked forward to this day in anticipation of my chocolates. My husband humored me for a few years and then one day informed me that Valentines Day was not a Jewish holiday, but indeed a "goyisha" (non-Jewish) holiday celebrating the memory of St. Valentine. He quickly informed me that not only does the Torah forbid our celebrating certain non-Jewish holidays, but there was a "Jewish Valentines day" and it is Tu B'av, the 15th of Av. I quickly informed him that that was really nice, but Hallmark was not aware, nor the chocolate companies.

At any rate, today, the 15th of Av (mid July and not mid February) is Tu B'av, and every year my husband faithfully remembers the day showering me with love and affection. Historically, Tu B'av was a joyous holiday in the days of the Temple in Jerusalem. Unmarried girls would dress in white clothing (so that the rich could not be distinguished from the poor) and go out to sing and dance in the vineyards surrounding Jerusalem. Young men, who had not yet married, would go to watch and choose a wife. The Talmud states that there were no holy days as happy for the Jews as Tu B'Av and Yom Kippur.

Although the day has no specific observances in modern times, it is considered an auspicious day for marriage. It also marks an informal "high" to counter the "low" of the Three Weeks. It is considered in modern times to, sort of, be a Jewish Valentine's Day, an optimal day for weddings, proposals, and romantic dates in Israel. So, why not buy roses and chocolate in July? Try out Tu B'av, which has origins dating back thousands of years. It sounds like Hallmark is missing out.

Proud to be an American

Red, White, Blue and a Jew

Ok, so truthfully I have to thank my sister-in-law, Amy for the suggestion for this blog. There's never a dull moment when we all get together and this occasion started out with my father's eightieth birthday celebration. The party was scheduled for July 4th at my parent's apartment complex. Planning this event was no small feat and took all four of us to pull it off. Having never thrown a celebration where the median age was seventy-five, we weren't sure how this would all work out. Aside from forgetting that one third of the attendees were wheelchair users (needing to be waited on and served), it was really a wonderful event. Having it occur on July 4th, meant that we would end our evening at Lenox Mall at the annual fireworks show.

Now, no one with any sanity goes to this event, as there are no less than 60,000 people crammed into a hot parking lot. Parking is pretty much a free-for-all and so anyone, with any sense, will park several blocks away to try to have an easier escape route at the end of the evening. We, of course, (my husband, boys and myself) stick out like, well, we just stuck out. My husband says,

108

"Someone just said 'rabbi' and pointed to me. How could they tell?" My brother-in-law proceeds to explain to him that, on July 4th, one of the hottest days of the year, no one wears long black pants and a long sleeve white shirt. My husband finds this startling and smiles.

We settle into our six foot by six foot spot (there are twenty of us) on the concrete with lawn chairs, food and games. We seem to prefer the "close up" spot where left overs from the fireworks fall on your head, as opposed to the back of the parking lot where you would be deafened by the band. It's a hard choice, but our traditional spot is under the rain of firework ashes. We are always grateful when it doesn't actually rain, as we have spent some years huddling under a tarp, too wise to get up and leave. Anyway, behind us is a man with a pit-bull (one does wonder) and next to us is a family whose son has a mohawk (I want to rub my fingers through it, but resist the urge). I ponder the difference between this warrior haircut and my boys who look more like goats. Now that we are comfortable amongst "friends" (and close enough to get to know them too well) and feeling so proud to be a part of the USA, we wait.

This part is actually fun as we joke, laugh, play games, eat. Of course, there is the dreaded trip to the porto-potties. There are about twenty-five of them lined up, and we actually wait to use them. There is nothing quite as grotesque as using a porto-potty in a parking lot. Yet, there is some sort of demented comfort knowing that twenty-five others are using it with you. I am pretty sure it is a fireworks event-right-of-passage to experience relieving oneself in a box sitting in the middle of a parking lot. It eventually gets dark and is time for the fireworks (after my son has asked me fourteen times what time it is) and they are breathtaking! Yes, the firing is something close to a sonic boom and makes one unsure whether you are having a cardiac arrest, but I have found that if you plug your ears it helps. And, wearing sunglasses prevents the fall-out and smoke from getting in your eyes. So, another year, blessed to be with family:) Happy Birthday Aba! May you live to 120 and God bless the USA.

Where's Your Turkey

I was recently shopping at Trader Joe's to pick up some fresh items to add to our Shabbos dinner. I was watching the gawking checkout lady (she was amazed at the amount of food I was purchasing). Then came the comment: "Getting ready for Thanksgiving? Well, I don't see a turkey here." I started to explain that this purchase was not for Thanksgiving, but for a regular Sabbath meal. I decided to just cut my losses and said, "No. I haven't bought the turkey yet." She then let me know that I had better get one soon. After so many years of feeding the religiously hungry population a few times each month, I find it amusing that a Thanksgiving meal is such a production to most people. I don't belittle the significance or the quality time spent with family, because other than hundreds of thousands of dead wild life and the fact that the Native Americans were robbed of their land, it's really a feel-good, be-good holiday. I suppose if I only had an extended family/friend meal twice each year, it would be a huge deal to me too, but as my happy Hasidic hubby likes to remind me, every day is Thanksgiving when you're Jewish.

Well, I did purchase my turkey and set my hubby to cooking it (which he artfully has mastered over the years, not from Thanksgiving, but from Rosh Hashanah, Pesach, etc.). Our daughter phoned home and said she was expecting a full-Thanksgiving fare, southern style. No way we could pass up the request. We enjoyed our turkey and the rest of the traditional foods, but mostly we enjoyed each other. We ate our turkey on Friday night during our

Shabbos dinner when we gave thanks, not only for our Shabbos meal, our week and a multitude of other things, but also for the fact that our bird died exclusively to be eaten at a Shabbos table.

Teach Your Children Well

"Men talk about the holiness of God and there is no peace. They talk about the holiness of other men and still no peace. Ah, but when the mashiach comes and men talk about the holiness of children, then there will be peace." Rabbi Shlomo Carlebach

We are part of an Orthodox community. That means we are part of a community with a lot of children, God bless their parents... and the rest of us. These children grow and they become part of our community. Sometimes these children are cute and adorable and sometimes they are knocking over Kiddush tables and climbing the walls like little Tasmanian devils. It is a different philosophy, families having multiple babies, than the standard American 1.86 children per household. This comes with its blessings and with its challenges. One of our rabbis once relayed the following story to me. He was standing at a checkout after purchasing a week's worth of food for his family of eight children (ages nine and under) when the check out lady said, "Oh are you having a party?" He replied, "No. I have eight children." To which the checkout lady said, "Oh." To which our rabbi said, "Oh?..... Are you wondering how I manage?" She said, "Well, yes." She was probably wondering a lot more. He said, "How many children do you have?" She said, "One, and I find him hard to handle." Our rabbi said, "You have expectations. We don't have many expectations in regards to our children or ourselves. No expectations of sleeping, personal time or quiet. Our children are our focus and so we are happy and high on living; whatever comes our way we will handle. So, we are never disappointed."

I have been over this rabbi's house and he is right. His eight children have very little and are very happy, as are he and his wife. I, like many others, was not raised without expectations and for sure that has been a challenge for Mordechai and me. Yet, I had a taste of this story when I was pregnant with twins and I would get comments like, "Oh, do you know what you got yourself into?" Or "I'm glad they are yours and not ours." It made me realize how "me centered" our society is, a culture where comfort is a priority. Even if one doesn't have eight children, we would be much more content if we become a bit more "you" focused. I'm not suggesting that people should have huge families, but maybe our priorities just need a shift.

The first time I laid eyes on my oldest son, Lev, I had an instant feeling of inadequacy, as if I couldn't do enough for him. I really didn't know the first thing about taking care of a baby, which was evident within just a few minutes of his birth. But, he taught me well. Aside from dropping him off a month early at camp one summer and putting him in a ballet recital (I thought it would be good for his coordination), with a sprained ankle, we did okay. Yet, at the moment of his birth, the rest of the world instantly became way too large for such a tiny infant. He had such a knowing look, that of a little old man. It felt as if he were an old soul, who had come to show me my way around. From day one, Lev was intuitive, creative, funny and kind hearted. To this day, I believe that is his core. I just assumed everyone could see those gifts, and that everyone would want to foster those God-given strengths. I saw myself more as his facilitator endowed with the privilege of learning how to parent him. Ultimately, he would change me far more than I would change him. I did not see myself as his director. That was not my job. Nope, I was going to be a supportive, cool, understanding parent. I never anticipated that my husband or the educational system might have an agenda for him or my other three children. In fact, each child brought me lessons in parenting, marriage and education different from each of their siblings.

One thing I'm sure of is that our kids must have often wondered if they had been swapped at birth, and their *real*, religiously-in-sync-parents were out there somewhere. I was blind-sided by Mordechai's passion to Orthodoxy. It crept up on me and my children, somewhat like... a bubble bath turned tsunami. Honestly, there were times we all felt sucked into a vacuum. Perhaps it was a good vacuum, but it was for sure a strong pull. My older kids transitioned with us into a more observant lifestyle, often taking the brunt of our over or under zealousness or confusion. I have promised them years of therapy in return. I had one foot in my idealistic view of education and child rearing and my big toe dipped into a religious view. They didn't match up too often. My children were placed in a system where every day they were reminded that they were created in the image of God and that the choices they made were not just for now, but for eternity. I'm just not sure that we as parents translated that to them with all the rules and rituals. Baal Teshuvas can sometimes get too focused on details and lose perspective. The first time I even heard about being created in the image of God as a way of viewing myself was at the age of thirty-two, and it didn't really register, even then. I was just trying to figure out how to survive being observant and being married.

If we ever disagreed over anything while being married it was only minor, just how to raise and educate our children. My vision of our children was that of blue-jean-t-shirt-wearing kids getting in touch with their God-given gifts. I wanted a "light" Jewish education for my children, topped with many "feel-good" experiences like holidays, matzah ball soup, Jewish overnight camp, sports, music lessons and a few good secular holidays. Add in some hiking trips, creative schooling and hugs and you have yourself a well-bred American Jew. I coveted good, quality education and real camp. I wanted my kids to be at the center of their experiences and education that put my kids at the center. I had a lot to learn. My problem was that I actually had expectations. I don't think they were too high.

Anyway, the education that was available to my children in Atlanta, within the confines of an Orthodox day school, required a lot of compromise and change of priorities on our part. We had four choices of Jewish day schools and my husband eliminated two of them right away. The third was the

114

Orthodox day school; and, the fourth he would eventually settle for, as a compromise, and compromises of this form never really work.

My husband, unbeknownst to me, had his eye on raising little Yeshiva "bochurs" (boys who learn in a traditional yeshiva system) and a "bochurette." It's not a bad concept; it's just that I wasn't really aware of his concept. Call me clueless. Our two concepts were so far removed from one another that it was a far reach to discuss them in the same conversation. It wasn't that my husband didn't also want quality education, it's just that he was a bit blind-sided by his own journey and willing to forgo other educational goals for Torah education. I will humbly say that I was willing to forgo Torah education, for lack of a better term, for "whole-child" education.

I remember my first teacher conference for Lev where the teachers handed me a picture drawn by Lev. He had been asked to color in a menorah. He had scribbled red crayon all over the page. They explained to me that his artwork was immature. So, I took the paper home to Lev and asked him why he had scribbled all over the paper in red. He looked me straight in the eye and said, "Mommy, the menorah caught on fire." I thought back to the conference and realized that they had missed so much about his picture and about him. In addition I had "new parent syndrome," where I expected my child's gifts and abilities to be recognized. Why was God making it so hard for me to buy into this system? Where was the Orthodox day school that was going to educate *my* son?

I saw the kids who excelled in this system, yet I also saw kids who fell through the cracks of Orthodox day school education. It seemed like it would take a miracle to avoid the trap. This system seemed to produce some well prepared kids, yet a number of kids would come out of high school without the skills or preparation to go onto higher education. One parent said to us, "Don't worry. Just put them in at kindergarten and hold your breath. They all come out the other end." It felt like we had fallen into a spiral. I felt no way out, as I was choosing between our religious ideals and good secular education for our children. I could see many "unlaunched" children: twenty-something-year-olds, married, with children of their own, supported by their parents and not knowing how to fend for themselves.

This was disconcerting to me. This wasn't just about money. It was about self worth and contribution, which, from my perspective, only came from higher education. It took me years to see the value of this system that may not be measurable from our current standards. Perhaps, the traditional definition of success, that I had grown up with, was not lasting; but how could so many unemployed people be supported? My parents had struggled financially, and, so, I had made sure that I would be financially independent, of *anyone*. But, maybe we are not supposed to be independent of one another? Perhaps, I needed to re-evaluate my priorities? Perhaps I needed to just trust the system, to trust my children, to trust God? Honestly, I wasn't doing too well in this department.

Yeshiva or Bust

This past week one of our rabbis was explaining that the weekly Torah portions, up until this point, were captivating and easily peeked one's interest, as they were mostly in a story format. Now, he explained, we were reading the portions that deal with all the mitzvot. He further explained the necessity of having rules to live by. He then went on to tell us why often, for example, an inmate will (after being released) commit a crime simply to return to the structure and routine provided by living in prison. He is provided with routine, camaraderie and three meals a day. I couldn't help but ask," So, what is the difference between a prison and a yeshiva?" He smiled and told me he'd get back to me on that subject a bit later.

This seems to be a sensitive subject lately: Who works and who learns? Are the learners really learning? or is the comfort of the learning routine and three meals a day the attraction? For sure there is comfort in routine. I like routine. It provides a certain rhythm. I happen to have a son in yeshiva. He knows he cannot stay there forever, and, yet, just the other day he remarked to me how comforting the routine has become for him. I have heard the same from soldiers returning from service. The change in routine and pace was the most difficult adjustment. So, how does one get out of a rut or are we meant to be creatures of habit?

Anyway, my son came home for the sukkot break from his Yeshiva. It took me three weeks to de-program him and re-orient him to the real world, where people make eye contact and greet each other with socially acceptable words, work for a living, mow the lawn, pick up trash, empty dishwashers, exercise and go on hikes. After we embarrassed him a few times and nagged him a few hundred times, he caught on. He's quite bright (and

handsome too), so the deprogramming only took a couple of weeks. We went into high alert when he told us he wasn't sure how long he would be in Yeshiva, four years, six years, indefinitely? We put in a direct call to the "all alert potential failure to launch" vocational adviser, which caused him to suffer through several hours of intense "what is my five year plan" surveys and counseling. This was followed by a day at a home health care exhibition trade show in Atlanta where he met working people. By the end of the three weeks, he even remarked about the beautiful trees that he was leaving behind in Atlanta. That is when I knew my job was complete (for this session).

It is not that I'm opposed to the scholarly type, but, well, someone has to feed them. Now, his little brother, who prefers to read the Little Midrash Says to playing soccer, might just fit the role of a full-time Torah scholar one day. And, my daughter, well, let us all pray that she is "found" soon, as she is aspiring to be a film star. This is all baffling my reasonable and responsible approach toward life. At least one of my four kids needs to earn some money at some point, please God. We've asked for a dentist, and so far none of our children are aspiring to be one. Go figure.

Meanwhile, it's back to Brooklyn for my oldest. It's back to black and white, all day learning, asphalt, snow, yeshiva bochurs (young men), rebbes and this very different world than the one I grew up in. Maybe that's not so bad. It feels quite scary to me and yet maybe the traditional path is even scarier. Who knows? Next break? Pesach. I'm already preparing his debriefing. Maybe the fact that I've ejected him out of his room and boxed it up might help him see the need for future financial security. Well, I have time. Plus I'm planning a mid–February visit to his Yeshiva. In the meanwhile, I think I'll send him some flowers for Chanukah. Should brighten up his Yeshiva just a bit.

Like any good parent, I realized my children's potentials, but when it came to education, I relied on the school. I learned quickly that the way I was educated was not going to work for my own children. I had to get involved. When I realized Lev was slipping through the system, we moved both him and Carmelle to the community Jewish day school that Mordechai and I had attended. Our children received an improved secular education, but they were also more religiously isolated. So, in middle school, we moved Lev back to the Orthodox Jewish day school. These were confusing times for all of us, and we added two more children to the mix, our twins, Rafi and Nissim, and put them in a preschool at a local Conservative synagogue. So, our kids now had a Hasidic father, hippie-trendy mother, Lev was at an Orthodox Jewish day school, Carmelle was right smack in her tween years at a community Jewish day school and the twins were at a Conservative preschool. I do not recommend what we did as a model, for anyone. Do *not* try this at home. We, for sure, gave them something to be confused about so they didn't have to go too far to find it.

Mordechai would always remind me that it wasn't our children's Yiddishkite, their Jewish identity, which concerned him; rather it was our grandchildren's Yiddishkite that concerned him. If you kept your eye on your grandchildren, the decisions were easy. But, most of us, myself included, have a hard time seeing the forest through the trees. I supported the goals to instill Yiddishkite. I just had difficulty seeing how the system supported my educational goals. The kids seemed spent, exhausted and often burnt out. We were spending astronomical amounts to support this system. There almost seemed to be a fear of allowing the children time to pursue anything else. But, what if this system doesn't work? I kept asking this question and I was assured many kids made it through the system well prepared for other avenues. What if they couldn't find those un-tapped talents twelve years later?

There were times I felt that I had put my kids on an assembly line and so to survive I had become an unconscious parent, justifying why this system was the best way to educate Jewish children. Looking back, I'm not sure I would have chosen any other way. Today my twins are in another Orthodox Jewish day school. Change is never easy. My expectations are also lower. In addition, we are all starting to understand that education is complex and is much more than curriculum. Our children are multi-faceted people. That understanding has taken some time. Our children, as well as Mordechai and myself, have for sure been a part of that discovery.

When our twins reached kindergarten, we decided to put them into public school (a huge cost savings for a couple years) and we home-schooled them in Judaics. Overnight, I became an instant kindergarten teacher, teaching them parsha, Hebrew, songs and art projects. Then, in second grade, we put them into the religious school (armed and prepared to hire tutors or supplement the secular education) and most importantly to be involved with their education. I became the most supportive, cheerleader-director-teacher-mom I knew how to be. I knew what I wanted from the school. I knew the schools limitations and I went in prepared to support. Once again, I had to change expectations.

School Daze

Today all our neighborhood kids went off to school. It was hard for me to watch them. My twins spent the past two years at the neighborhood school where their secular education was of no worry. They met friends like Kyoto, Gichan, Jake and Minishweenie. The teachers were kind and professional. Everyday they were excited to see my boys and the entire system ran like clockwork. I will miss our walk to school across the lakeside path, across the bridge with rushing waters below and by the playground (our afternoon stop). My dog will miss her friends, Eddie, Sadie Maye, Ginger and Lulu and barking at the school buses. I will miss all the friends we met. With their kippas and payos (side locks) they were accepted among the diverse school culture. And, yet, secular influences can have their toll.

This year my boys will be going to Jewish day school. I have put two other children through this experience, so I am not new at this. It comes with a price. My boys will have friends named Yosef Chaim, Chaim Yitzchak and Shmuel Yaacov. Instead of walking we will wait in the carpool line (my dog will hang her head out the window and snarl at the rabbis). There will be a plethora of wild Jewish children who don't have parties on Saturdays....well, who don't have parties and don't leave their neighborhood.

But....There will also be rebbeim, Jewish songs, Jewish holidays and ....TORAH. We will NOT make gingerbread houses that you do not eat (I never quite caught onto that). Instead, they will learn to make a mishkan (tabernacle). We cannot put a price on any of this. Well, actually, yes we can. We will be exchanging what was simple, well run and FREE for what is haimish, expensive, authentic, and ours. It's the price we pay for our future. Well, here's to a great year. May the sacrifice be small, the rewards great, the children well behaved, the teachers professional and the Torah palpable. Maybe I should just pray for the Mashiach.

So, I had to recalibrate when it came to my dreams of educating my children and even for raising them. The truth is that like most issues, the problem was a disconnect between my needs and the system, that, truth be told, worked fine for many other families and children. I also had a lot to learn about parenting myself. Maybe the entire experience was a lesson for me?

Most parents want what's best for their children. I wanted my kids to soar. Who doesn't? I wanted inspiration. I wanted motivation. I wanted great education. In Hebrew the word to teach is "melamed" and is a reflexive form of the word to learn: "lamed." You cannot have one without the other. I learned so much from watching my children go to school and receive an education. As a partner in their education, I learned about them, about myself and a lot about our education system. And, the system learned a lot about parents like me who want more than curriculum and a certified teacher. I think if we are to create tomorrow's leaders, we have to engage today's students. To teachers who do that (and I know you do), I applaud you. Kids today are smart, savvy, technologically literate (beyond what most of us can ever imagine), and, well, our work is cut out for all of us: parents, teachers and children. I also believe that all children *want* to learn. It takes a team approach of good parenting, teaching and love.

Camp or Bungalow Babysitting?

My twins are at overnight camp for the first time. This is not the first time I've sent children to overnight camp, but the first time at an all boy's religious Orthodox overnight camp in the Catskills. Apparently, it is an extension of the NY Bungalow Colonies and culture. I did not get the memo. I chose this camp because 1) it was Orthodox 2) it was all boys 3) it had a great facility and 4) it had a great website. I suppose that doesn't add up to much, but I did interview the director; and it has been around for twenty-five years... So, I figured it couldn't be all too bad. And, truth be told, it is a pretty good camp. It's organized, has good food and good learning. In addition, it has a great facility. Darn those expectations! Apparently, all the boys brought their "DS" to camp. Silly me. I thought when it said, "no electronics" that it meant "no electronics." It seems that it said, "no DSI" but not "DS." Seriously?? So instead of the boys engaging with one another, they disengage. When they are not "wired," they are learning, eating or being entertained. It also seems we are supposed to tip our counselors at the mid point of the session. Huh? That's like tipping your waiter after the soup. I'm trying to figure out exactly what I'm tipping for.

In addition, I did not receive the "bring hot kugel to your son weekly, if not more often, and dress up in your fanciest outfit when you show up" memo. My husband went up for visiting day and he informed me that this was no Camp Barney. At Camp I learned to make a "zero impact" campfire. I learned to ride horses. I learned to swim and passed four levels under the American Red Cross. I learned to water ski. But most importantly, I learned what it was like to live without television (no DS, Ipad, Iphone, Iwhatever), without air conditioning and without mom and dad. No phone calls. No visiting day and...No hot kugel. Enough said. I'm confident that by the end of the summer, my boys will have grown up a lot, but I really wish parents would NOT send your kids to camp with their electronics. Really. The kids will be okay.

Aside from our children's education, I struggled with how to embrace my children's own unique needs within the confines of orthodoxy. I particularly felt this angst with our daughter, who had a passion for the stage and wanted to audition for television and films. There are many restrictions within orthodoxy that are in conflict with being a performer. Mordechai actually wanted her to get an agent to audition, yet I did not want to see her struggle with conflicts that would arise between acting and being observant. I also wanted to present her with the right intentions for being on stage. Attention for the wrong reasons would not last, nor be meaningful and could be dangerous in the long run. At times it was painful to watch her go through this struggle. Yet, this struggle has also helped her find some very meaningful and often entertaining ways of using her talent. One example of this was a YouTube video she made called, "Shdus Baalei Teshuva Say." It not only shows her talent, but her understanding of the Baalei Teshuva World. Today there are many more opportunities to express oneself creatively via film or theater within the orthodox world. I suspect she will carve her own path.

At any rate, one thing I knew was that if she was going down this path with us, to become a strong confident woman, she had to make some decisions of her own. Mordechai and I often argued over the way she dressed. Whereas, he felt that I should enforce a dress code, I wanted her to choose it. I also wanted her to choose observance for herself. I felt that being pressured would backfire. So, as she made her way through high school, I kept offering her a chance to go learn Torah in Israel, something I had never had the chance to do. Because, with observance, comes education. You cannot have one without the other.

Seminary or Bust!

My daughter is looking for a seminary to attend next year in Israel. This is a new experience for all of us. For those of you who don't know what that is, it is a religious learning environment for post-high school girls that usually lasts a year. It gives them a chance to spend that year learning religious studies in depth and to grow up a bit before heading off to college (or for some before they get married). It is a "gap" year. It is also a gift.... from their parents....an expensive one. Representatives from many of the seminaries have visited my daughter's school, and she has had the opportunity to interview with them. They all love her. What is not to love? She is cute, smart, has great Judaic skills and is outgoing. I'm thinking that maybe they should pay us for her to attend. Anyway, she is torn between many of the schools. Each time one comes to visit, it is her favorite.

The other night she put them all up on our wipe erase board and wrote down her pros and cons. It seems that each one has a slightly different dress code (aka: lenient or stringent) and, thus, is more or less religious (all on a very gray scale). In listening to all her pros and cons, she consistently pointed out the "dress." After all, whether your sleeves are above the elbow or below the elbow, whether your skirts are above the knee or below the knee, and what you wear in class versus after class will surely (according to her) have a lifetime affect on you. After weeks of her deliberating and my husband inquiring about the classes, teachers, activities and locations, he had an epiphany. He suggested that she go to her wardrobe (if she can pick it all off the floor and that only occurs about twice a year), and decide, based on her current offering, which seminary she is currently outfitted for. This seemed simple to him and made sense to me as well.

But, then what would the point of a shopping spree be? Meanwhile, we have donated to each seminary's application process and we wait and see. I have the feeling I'm going to have to go buy a new wardrobe, luggage, and a plethora of personal items, because it seems that she and her friends have decided that deodorant and other personal items simply cannot be purchased in Israel. She needs to buy a year's worth of these things here and schlep them across the Atlantic. Maybe she will meet a nice soldier to carry her bags when she gets there, because no one else will be able to lift her wardrobe and personal gear. I have a feeling she is going to be schlepping a bunch of Israeli products back here as well. It looks like I'm going to be paying on both ends either way.

My heart goes out to all of my children and to those children of other BT parents. Please know that we do not intend to ever control, manipulate or embarrass you. Our constant change in dress code, hairstyle and rituals (as well as those we've impressed upon you) are only intended to "recalculate" so that we may join the mission of the Jewish people, and, as a bonus, to provide you with entertainment as you retell our story to future generations. As much as we have tried to present you with a love of Torah, we for sure have often been misguided by our passion or confusion. We only pray that you will reap the rewards of having being brave "army brats," and please do repay us with armfuls of grandchildren.

Matchmaker Matchmaker Make Me a LOAN

Recently on a visit home from Yeshiva my son informed us that when the time arrives that he is ready to marry, there would be several fees involved. Upon the previous visit he informed us about FLOPS: flowers, liquor, orchestra, photography and sheitel responsibilities to be paid by the grooms side of the family. He is quite good about dropping these bombs on his innocent, BT- hard-working parents in small increments. He did not read us or provide any "fine print" or disclaimers regarding other hidden fees, although we are sure they were hidden somewhere in the conversation. Anyway, this past visit he explained to us the matchmaker (shadchan) fee. Huh? But you won't need a matchmaker, we explained. You are young, handsome and with great social skills, and we will just "put the word out" when you are ready to date (Okay, well, maybe your not so religious relatives, Hassidic-modern Orthodox-dog owning family, and the fact that you have no career plans at this time, might make you just a bit less of a marriage candidate). He then explained that it really doesn't matter. Even if a friend, rabbi, acquaintance or some homeless person off the street recommends a potential bride, you have to pay a matchmaker fee. Huh? Seriously? Am I hearing right? We actually pay someone who says "I know a nice girl for you?" Do you mean we owe back payment to the woman who set my husband and I up in 3rd grade to do our spelling assignment together? I mean where does it stop? Is there no honor anymore in word of mouth favors? And, he was not talking about a small fee.

I mulled this all over in my head and decided that perhaps we needed to be doing some matchmaking ourselves. It was quite the lucrative business. But, then I came up with an idea for the rest of the unsuspecting baalei teshuva parents out there. Why not just set up an on-line service and by pass the matchmaker? We could call it lowfeematchmaker.com! For $49.99 you get as many dates as you need! I was informed that existed already and that it was not the real-deal. At this point, I asked my son if he had considered eloping when the time comes. He looked at me with that look. He was not going to change the system. He knew he had time on his side. His mother would eventually come around...or provide a very untraditional fee/gift when (God willing) the time will come. I have been known to be quite creative. If nothing else, I know a cute girl next door.

Travelling Like a Yid

"Go from your land, from your birthplace, and from your father's house, to the land that I will show you."
(Genesis: 12:1)

Our observance picked up pace throughout the years and it not only impacted our daily lives but our off-scheduled times as well. What always amazed me was that my husband would run into a religious Jew no matter where we travelled. He was like a magnet to them. We never left home without an entourage of suitcases filled with his bekeshas, books, and tefillin and, of course, hat boxes. In addition, we had a cooler and several grocery bags of kosher food. I would pack up the car, and he'd then add three more suitcases. There were also issues with when we could travel.

As previously mentioned, the nine-days are a restrictive time due to many past tragedies, so travelling during that part of the summer, although an ideal season, is not an ideal time. There are restrictions such as not swimming, not listening to music and so on. There is also the decision as to where to travel that fits our lifestyle. But, the biggest change for me early on was not eating out when on vacation, as many places did not have kosher establishments. In truth, I came to enjoy the eating-in on vacation, especially with kids. It was actually much less of a hassle than hunting down a child friendly restaurant every night. Did I miss the restaurant experience? Maybe just a bit, but we managed to find a few kosher establishments, and we also managed to involve our kids from time to time in the planning and cooking.

As soon as we realized that our kids had gone on "vacation" and we were experiencing more of a "working family trip," we decided that they would need to help out with the food. Two of my favorite vacations were our RV trip and our camping trip. I planned and executed these trips against, what seemed like, an army of rebelling teenagers, but the outcome was, well...amusing. And, of course, there is no describing a trip to Israel. It's just that my yearning for the land and my husband's yearning for people in black suits often created some strife in the planning process. In the end, though, we loved our trips, and aside from leaving our little dachshund behind, we all gave them a thumbs up! I'm still waiting to travel across the country. I love the open road. My husband is not in favor, but the jury is still out. He knows, though, that I will plan it. Then he will re-plan it. And, then we will go.

RV Yeshiva

This past week we went on an RV trip, our first RV trip. I have wanted to do this for many years and my family finally acquiesced and agreed to a short three day RV trip to Tennessee. Of course, we brought along the necessities for any religious family going on an RV trip: Torah books, prayer books, tefillin and a plethora of kosher food.

Day 1: As we were packing up our van (to go pick up the RV) my son Rafi (age seven at the time) says, "The neighbors are awake and they might see all this stuff and think we are moving!" We leave the house at 8:00 a.m. (with a van full of kosher food, bags, enough stuff to fill an RV, plus six people), and my husband says, "It is still not too late to back out of this trip." My eighteen-year-old son comes out of the house and says, "Are we going to the beach? To Yellowstone?" At which time my sixteen-year-old daughter says, "How many rooms does the RV have?" At 9:30 a.m., we are in the RV parking lot (being oriented to our "home" for the next three days). Three of us need to use the restroom. We're afraid to use the bathroom in the RV. The owner of the RV has warned us not to make sharp right turns or we might pull off a stop sign, curb, telephone pole, etc. It is a monstrosity, all thirty-five feet of it. At 12:00 noon we pull into a gas station. We scrape the bottom of the RV.

At 1:00p.m. we stop at some caverns. We spend two hours in a damp moist cave, 300 feet underground and learn about how long it takes to go blind in the dark. We are informed about the woman who was once left behind and climbed up the cave stairs in the dark. We are all now feeling warm and fuzzy. We are also informed that the oxygen is 30% less and that last week 800 people had a party in the cave. I can't think of a more miserable place to have a party. At 5:45 p.m. we hook up to our campsite. I have a headache and only one Motrin on me. I venture out with my daughter to beg for another Motrin from the "neighbors." They are toothless, but manage to understand my needs, and I am relieved to acquire four more Motrin.

At this point, my teenagers are huddled under the A/C vent and won't move. They fight for the A/C spot in the RV while the rest of us sweat. Everything in the RV is little: little water, little air, little beds, little cupboards, just plain little. My husband ventures out to find a can opener, of course to later be kashered, and to meet more neighbors. He asks our closest neighbor, "So how long have you been here?" The man answers with a southern twang "Oh, about two weeks." My husband says, "In this spot?" The man says, "Yep. Right in this spot." My husband comes back baffled at the thought of staying in one spot at a campsite for two weeks. It makes me think that many of us, perhaps, get stuck in one spot. Change is hard. 8:00 p.m.: We drive down to visit the lake. We are alone there, and it is beautiful. We go wading in the water. We are now very wet. My daughter asks, "Don't we have a dryer?"

Day Two: We venture out of our "spot." The neighbors are bewildered by the fact that we move in and out so frequently. We stop by the "dumping station." We all back up (way back as we've seen the movie "RV") while my husband empties the "pipe." It makes a horrible gurgling sound, and we are all amazed. We seal up and are on our way when we smell a horrible stench and are forced to stop. Seems like we left a valve open. We close it. Quickly. We go on a beautiful, waterfall hike and then to a swimming hole where my husband insists that we act like the yokels, hang with the yokels and jump from cliffs. We all refuse. I finally agree and get water up my nose: another reminder not to agree so often. My son is deciding at this point that RVs are not a good investment. At night, we cook out on an open fire and roast marshmallows. I am happy.

Day Three. We visit another park and go horseback riding. I decide that my legs are not designed to straddle a horse. We spend another peaceful day lugging our home *around Tennessee, hiking to waterfalls and swimming in secluded water holes. We cook another dinner and roast marshmallows. Grace, our seven-year old neighbor, asks my twins to play. They play hide and seek around the bathhouse. She is here with her aunt and grandparents, and they have not moved in two weeks. She visits the nature center (a 6' x 6' building) as an "outing." Grace informs us that she prays nightly for a brother or sister. My boys cannot relate. It starts to drizzle and we welcome the rain.*

Day Four: We travel home. My sister informs me of her friend who lost their $500 RV deposit thirty minutes before returning their RV, when they ripped the roof off on a gas station awning. I keep this in mind as we head back. I pray we don't rip the roof off any gas stations before we return the beast back home. We make it. I give thanks. I could do this trip again. However, I have been outvoted.

Beach Trip

This summer we decided to take a beach vacation, as it was clear that no one was going with me on a repeat RV vacation. So, off we headed to Ormond Beach, Florida, a quiet beach a few miles north of Daytona. The day before we left was Tisha B'av, a fast day. This meant we really could not pack (too weak from fasting to lift my arms, much less a suitcase) until late that night. We were traveling with seven people (two adults, two teens, two eight-year-olds plus my mother-in-law...she had priority seating) in a minivan. You are now trying to imagine how we all fit into a minivan. While you are doing that, try to imagine all of us, plus my sister and brother in law (who visited us), staying in a two-bedroom condo. It can be done! Everyone was instructed to bring no more than one SMALL bag that fits in the "foot-space under their seat" or in the "overhead compartment" (bag on top of the car).

Yes, there was a small revolt from my teenagers ("I can't be an outfit repeater!" and "How will I fit all my electronics?"). Of course, we had to bring a couple of boogie boards, a skim board, Torah books, tefillin, etc. I am not sympathetic to "over-packers," so I ignored these outbursts, realizing that the result of not following my instructions would be very cramped legroom and not a real problem for me as the primary driver (I managed to keep myself in that seat for most of the trip).

Our next issue was that my teens, who have spent the last eight plus years in the third row of the van during any family outings, decided that this year they would demand "middle row" seats. I acquiesced. Not twenty minutes into our drive, our oldest son said (at 5:45 a.m.), "I don't have anywhere to rest my head in the middle row." It seems like his early morning nap had been uprooted by a lack of head support. Oh, how I love letting the natural order of consequences occur. By 6:30 a.m. everyone was "adjusted" and grossly engaged in a personal electronic. No license tag games, no talking, no singing, no highway ABC games that I grew up with, just plug in and "zombify" your way to the beach. Silence is golden. How, I owe so many techno geeks for providing my children with technology addiction. Laura, our GPS, directed us to our destination without any disturbance from her passengers.

Our first stop at the beach was the Food Lion. Although we brought some kosher items with us, we needed to purchase the items that we did not schlep with us. I was pretty sure this Food Lion had never had an Orthodox Jewish family purchase a week's worth of food. Our plan was that each family member would be responsible for a day's meals. This went over about as well as "you need to clean up your room," but we would not relent! Anyway, as we approached the checkout and the cashier eyed our two overflowing buggies, she paged *over the loudspeaker, "I need help at checkout #3." She looked distressed. The bagger was panic-stricken. $300 later we left Food Lion with a weeks worth of "kosher" food and a beautiful beach waiting for us. That night we ate out at the one kosher restaurant on Ormond Beach. We were exhausted from grocery shopping.*

During the week, we went jet skiing (mom and younger boys on slow speed; dad and teens on lightening speed), surfing (well some of us...I tried but got swallowed up by a wave, and I have a wound on my knee to prove it!), boogie boarding (my husband insists on closely monitoring the wave quality so he can perform his 360 on the boogie board), skim boarding, swimming, playing putt-putt and a visit to Baskin Robbins. We even made a trip to the 7-11 for slurpies and were spotted by a couple other "yids." They saw us and said, "What's in Daytona? You must be going to the 7-11 for slurpies!" I mean, why else would Jewish people be at a 7-11? Our down time was spent playing cards and side-by-side technology usage.

My husband also brought us home a lonesome wave rider to join us for breakfast. He will never pass up on opportunity to meet someone new or rescue a lost soul. As my kids said, "Here comes Daddy with someone we don't know again."

And, thanks to my husband, my little Shabbos travel bag (candles, matches, wine, wine cup, havdallah candle and spices) and the Jerusalem café's catering our Shabbos meal, we were able to bring Shabbos to Ormond Beach. So, if there are sparks of holiness floating around, we gathered up some of them from Ormond Beach, Florida. Does that give us any brownie points? The New Year is coming up, and we can use some. It was such a great week and I am so grateful that what could have been an "un"vacation, became a real vacation. After all, a vacation where your kids feed you is something to be happy about.

Shabbos in San Fran

It is Friday evening. We are in a two-story condo in downtown San Francisco. My husband has chosen this urban, loud, smelly, dirty location because of its convenience to a very small shul, two blocks away. Our condo has become our home-away-from-home, and one of our favorite activities is people watching. We can see people getting ready for their "night-out," people walking, talking, shouting and homeless people talking to the walls. My husband and sons have returned from the Friday night services at the downtown shul. We are just about ready to start our Shabbos meal when we see a gathering down on the street near a small clothing shop. At this point, I say, "You know, Shlomo Carlebach would have invited those people in for a Shabbos meal."

Well, that's about all the encouragement my husband needed. He started toward the door when my teenagers say, "NO!" This "no" is only more encouragement to my husband. So, down he goes to the street (bekesha, black hat and all) and crosses over to the crowd. He is easy to spot. It has turned out that the clothing store is having their grand opening and is providing free music and beer. Free beer equals a lot of people. He approaches the first "brother" and says, "Hello, my holy brother, do you know any Jews in this crowd?" He is told there is one and he is pointed out. My husband, in an attempt to say what Shlomo would say, says, "My holy Jew! Good Shabbos! I really need a favor. You see, we are visiting from out of town. He then points up to the window where our six year olds were wide-eyed, looking out the window. The teenagers were hiding behind the wall and peering ever so inconspicuously out the side of the window, trying not to be seen. He then says, "It is the holy Shabbos and we are just about to make Kiddush and have our Shabbos meal. We are missing one thing, though. We have no guests. You would really save our lives if you would be our Shabbos guest for a little while." A few curious beer drinkers have gathered close to listen in on the invitation. They all start encouraging him to go. He asks if he can invite a friend who will be here in five minutes. My husband says, "Of course!" and puts up a hand showing five fingers. I am convinced he is bringing five people! He then invites this lost soul and his roommate up for Kiddush. It takes a bit of encouragement, but they come.

My little boys are giggling and my teens are trying to be unnoticed. Well, up come my husband, Eric and Jordan. They witness Kiddush and one tells us he thinks he has heard it before and that he recognized it. We make hamotsie (blessing over the bread), talk with them a while and then they decide to return to the safety of the street and free beer. Apparently, the word of the mysterious invite spread through the crowd. When my husband escorted them back across the street, the crowd breaks out in applause! We ponder this experience and wonder what impact if any this has had on them. Maybe none, maybe some or maybe the impact was on us. I know for sure, my children will remember this Shabbos well. Shlomo, we did you proud.

Camping Out

I grew up spending my summers in the mountains, so I am comfortable in the woods. This summer I decided I wanted a camping trip. I met up with a rebellion from my husband and daughter, who do not like to sleep anywhere other than a standard bed in an air-conditioned room. Our twins were actually happy to take part in the adventure. I shortened this "trip" to just one night so as not to cause too much trauma and purchased two tents:

one eight-man tent (hoping all six of us could fit in) and one four-man tent (in case my husband's snoring required that he have his own sleeping quarters). I spent a couple days gathering supplies, picked a state park not too far away and continuously warned everyone of our upcoming trip (they continued to be in denial).

The day arrived, and off we headed to Victoria Bryant State Park in the foothills of the Georgia Mountains. The Georgia Park brochure called it "Georgia's best kept secret."

We arrive to find out that we could select any of the eight tent platform sites (obviously, not too high of a demand for this best kept secret location). So, we chose one that had only one neighbor. They introduced themselves as "Debbie, Brent and our two sons." They seemed friendly enough. Brent said to my husband, "I think we are neighbors now." Honestly, I'm not sure Brent could say much more. Although he did inform us that he was from "nearby" (six miles nearby) and that this was their week-long vacation, an upgrade from last year's four-day vacation. I was humbled. My husband asked how long they had been in their site, and Brent replied, "We came for a week." We looked at their site and wondered what they had been doing or were going to do for a week at Victoria Bryant State Park.

Our first challenge was tent assembly. I prided myself in that I had watched the YouTube video. Only problem was the tent we had was just a wee bit different. We also didn't have a soft ground, but a hard, and I mean hard, platform. After a few failed attempts and nearly doubling over from laughter, my husband suggested that he read the instruction sheet. He managed to figure out how to assemble our new home.

As the evening rolled along, I crafted a killer meal of hamburgers, apples and banana boats (consisting of a banana sliced down the middle with marshmallows and chocolate stuffed inside and cooked over the fire). We soon became keenly aware that Debbie had some unique parenting skills (Brent didn't say much) that were quite different from our own. This became apparent when Debbie threatened to knock out her son's front teeth for getting soot on his shirt. They are staying in the woods for a week with a campfire and he got some dirt on his shirt. Wow. Talk about picking your battles. This didn't seem to faze her boys. In fact, several hours later she was still hollering, long into the night. I'm guessing, like most kids, Debbie's kids have tuned out her ranting and raving.

We managed to have a great fire and enjoy some fantastic night noises and then went off to bed (to the sound of Debbie's ranting and raving). As my husband lay down to sleep with his earplugs, yoga mat for padding, nice dose of Benadryl (and my children were complaining about the hard surface), I smiled listening to the summer bugs and being glad that every day I could say, "Thank God." Tonight I said a small prayer for Brent and his boys.

Soul Food

"And You Shall Eat and Be Satisfied" Deuteronomy 8:10 (God)

....but no creepy crawly things, Domino's® Pizza or Chick-Fil-A®

The first week we moved into our Dunwoody home I found an inspector rummaging through our pantry and checking labels like he was the executive chef of a five star restaurant.

It was my husband.

I had to suck him out of the pantry. The problem was he kept showing up in the kitchen. I had kept kosher my entire life, but it was obviously not up to my husband's current new standards. There seemed to be a few faulty hechshers (approved kosher labels) and it was his duty to rid our home of them. It was not exactly a problem; it was just that he forgot to mention this "free" upgrade to our new lifestyle. The kosher I was used to was one where I kept separate dishes, purchased kosher meat and cheese, but then didn't worry too much about boxed items. As a child there were not many hechshers, so people who kept kosher just read the ingredients. We ate out at restaurants. Candy, gum or ice cream was free for ingesting. Today there are different community standards and hechshers, enough to make someone insane. But, as a young girl, there was just one: an "O" with a "U" in the middle. Simple enough, so we thought.

It seems like my kosher and my husband's newfound kosher were from two different religions. As I would learn, fruits and vegetables, for example, needed to be inspected for bugs. If you want to scare an Orthodox Jew, just wave a piece of uninspected romaine lettuce. Also, many preservatives and food colorings are made from bugs and so you cannot rely on your own reading of ingredients.

Bug-Be-Gone

Orthodox Jews do not eat bugs. Period. It is forbidden. We are like religious exterminators with a mission to eradicate any and all bugs from the food industry, or at least from our own kitchens. It comes from the discussion in Leviticus (chapter 11) about the "winged swarming things" and "creepy crawly things." Apparently, some are kosher, but no one knows which ones, so they are all forbidden for fear of eating the ones we are not supposed to eat. Now, I am not a bug lover and have absolutely no desire to eat them, play with them, watch them, or analyze them. I honestly don't even get their purpose. Cockroaches, termites, slugs and other creepy crawly things pretty much gross me out. Anyway, this commandment gets a 10/10 on the obsessive commandment scale. Just the other day at a Shabbos meal, there was a bug discussion and my friend said, "Well, I'm going to get one of those bug lights." You see most bugs are really hard to see as they hide and camouflage themselves into the food. You would think that would make them okay to eat (being that you can't really see them), but not for us. Of course, this made everyone else at the table a bit nervous. Do I need a bug light? What if I miss a bug? What if her food is de-bugged better than my food? Will she eat my food that was checked without a bug light?

Either way, there are lots of buggies out there, and we have ways of checking for them. For example, you can hold lettuce up to any light and you may find a few bugs. These bugs are so small that you would never see them with the naked eye (unless you use a magnifying glass). We get really excited to find a bug, so we feel one step closer to our bug eradication mission. When I first became observant, I thought everyone was a bit crazy about this bug thing. I actually still do, sometimes, because at what level do you stop worrying? I mean, there are all sorts of microscopic bugs that we eat, breathe and ingest all day long.

Anyway, if you want to see a few bugs that you might normally not be noticing, try this technique for washing strawberries: cover them with water and a little dishwasher soap. See what floats to the top. Rinse and drain several times. Then cut off the tops (that's where the bugs live). Then know if you are eating at an observant household, you are probably getting just a bit less protein, but also the comfort of knowing you've ingested at least a few less bugs too. And, if you are newly observant and having guests over, you better check for bugs. Then throw in a discussion at the table about the bug you found, so everyone can breathe a sigh of relief and enjoy the holy food. Happy de-bugging.

Early in our observance Mordechai handed me a little card with about a hundred kosher symbols on it and told me that those were all approved and that I could purchase food with those symbols on the box or the package. Seriously? There was no way I'd remember every symbol. To this day, I only use about six of them as otherwise a trip to the grocery store would be more like an investigation. Even a pack of gum has to have a symbol on it. Keep in mind that our community, at the time, had a total of about four observant families. We were one of them, so whom he was worried about searching through our pantry, I cannot tell you. But, at that time it didn't seem like his concern was coming from a love for God, unless God had just stepped into our house that week. I could not understand his need to adhere so strictly to the kosher laws. I saw any kosher law as appropriate only if it worked with my current view or lifestyle... and was flexible. I never saw a kosher law as unwavering. I would come to realize (not soon enough) that attention to detail would surface frequently. He would ask me many times if something I bought was kosher (rightfully so, as I often would sneak in my favorite past times like gum or keep special "treats" in my car).

He had a right to be concerned, but I just couldn't keep up with his fervor, and honestly, I pined for the Domino's pizza man to show up at my door. He for sure delivered pizza in my dreams. I would drive by Chik-Fil-A just to get a whiff of a chicken sandwich. I was also being difficult; well, let's say I was a bit "slack" in the hechsher department. It took me many years to see halacha as an absolute and part of the entire landscape toward a relationship with the Almighty. All the kosher "software" was running down my hard drive. Mordechai was frequently checking the pantry; he admitted years later, when I wasn't around. I was frequently stuffing non-kosher food in my mouth when he wasn't around.

And, truthfully, I was beginning to not only miss Chik-Fil-A and the Domino's deliveryman, but I was also tired of having to think so hard... about *everything.* The food was just one piece of it. Waiting six hours after I ate meat was ruining my Haagen Daaz after dinner enjoyment. In addition, it was confusing, as there were people who only waited one hour, three hours or just spit and rinsed between meals. It seemed like if you didn't like a particular halacha, you could just say, "I don't hold by that." I would later come to really appreciate the discipline, but it was a few years down the road.

Kosher obsessive eating (something looked highly upon in my new world) would enter into every aspect of my life: visiting family, going to a bar-mitzvah celebration, going on vacation, preparing food on Shabbos (it is not kosher if not prepared properly ahead of time), holidays, business meetings, whose homes we would eat in, who would eat in our home and kid's birthday parties. Plus, I had to adjust to terms like Cholov Yisrael and Pas Yisrael (amongst a few other terms), which indicated an even stricter level of adherence to...something. I just wasn't always sure what. Even though I did not hold by those restrictions, many people in our community or friends of our children did, so it impacted us as well. In general, although I had grown up in a kosher home, this new level of kashrut required a lot more discipline and forethought.

Non-Kosher Events

So, an invitation would sometimes land in our mailbox. "Look", my husband says, "We can request kosher food at this event. Let's go!" It is not that we would go just for the food, but it was special when we could eat the food. It always seems really important to most hosts that we were able to partake. Now, I have been very blessed in that our extended families (as weird as they thought we were) were always very accommodating to our kosher restrictions. To this day, it always warms my heart how out of the way they will go to accommodate us (even if we are salivating over their slightly less kosher food). If we want to bring food, they are supportive. They are also very supportive to order kosher food for us. I know many families where this is a big problem, so I feel very fortunate. When an invitation would arrive and say, "kosher food available upon request." I would be thinking, "Oh no! Not the cellophane dinner!" You see, in order to ensure the strictest level of kashrut, the food is brought in from a kosher establishment and the food that is packaged for an event, is triple wrapped with a huge label indicating its strict adherence to kashrut. It might as well say, "This food is so well wrapped a nuclear bomb couldn't get to it." It almost felt like we were at one of those restaurants where someone at your table is celebrating their birthday and the restaurant comes over with noisemakers and a huge cake, drawing the attention of everyone else in the room. Our food would come out triple wrapped in cellophane with fourteen plastic utensils, an environmental travesty. Upon unwrapping this high-security meal, the beautifully set table would now have a huge mountain of cellophane as its centerpiece. Our tablemates would ask,"How is your salad different than ours?"

At this point, my teen-agers would slip away from the table to avoid being embarrassed by the oncoming discussion on kashrut. My husband would explain the basis for keeping kosher, which includes the prohibition from eating bugs that he would point out were probably in our tablemate's salad. Our tablemate would say, "Well, I don't eat bugs either," and my husband would then inform him how often he actually does or how many additives are made from bugs. Carmine is a red food coloring (it used to be labeled as red #4) that is made from ground up cochineal beetles. People eat it all the time.

This would enhance our table guests eating pleasure to no end. He would go into a lengthy discussion on the oral law, separating dishes, and cooking a kid in its mother's milk (a forbidden commandment in the Torah and the source for separating dairy from meat). Our tablemate would not own a kid (goat), and from the "Oh you poor people look," could not relate to this explanation. The poor man would be "trapped," but would listen with a look of confusion, interest and awe all mixed up. And, sometimes I often wonder if, for my next event, it would not be okay if I printed at the bottom of the invitation "non-kosher food available upon request."

How Kosher Is It?

Not too long ago my husband and I were invited to a religious event: a Torah dedication. My husband was the sofer (scribe) and was to attend as a special guest. I am usually happy to attend any sort of event as it usually means a night out, a good dinner with good entertainment and a nice social crowd. Most events we *attend are generally for a good cause as well, so we get our palettes tantalized while doing a good deed. As I entered this event, I saw tantalizing dishes of food, desserts, salads, drinks and my mouth was watering. My husband and I drove separately, so when I arrived, I went to find him.*

As I caught up with him, I said, "Did you see all the stations of food?" I obviously don't get out too much and was thrilled to be able to pick and choose from so many delicious looking choices. He informed me that the food was not kosher, and the hosts had kindly ordered kosher food for us. "Huh?" But we're at a religious event? It is even at a Conservative synagogue. How can the food not be kosher? You mean, I can't partake of the make your own chicken sandwich, the roast beef table, the fajita table, the dessert table, the create a salad table? I had already planned on my own creative "make your own chicken wrap," then the cute salad in a cup, followed by the chocolate dipped strawberries. Maybe I'd even go back for seconds! He explained that although the food was kosher-style, and he too had assumed it would be kosher, we could not eat it, as its supervision was skeptical (it was catered by a non-kosher restaurant). "Huh? (again)."

He then offered me a piece of matzah while we waited for our food. Well, it was Pesach Sheini (the remembrance of the Second Pesach for those during biblical times who had missed the first one), but seriously? I thought to myself, "Maybe I can adopt another husband, just for this event. No one will notice." But, then my good conscious berated me and said, "Be strong! You can do this!" So, I waited for my cellophane dinner.

You see there are so many levels of kosher that even within the world of kosher there are areas of gray. It has gotten all so confusing that one cannot assume that a pickle is kosher anymore.

One of our table guests commented, "Ah, I see you got the REAL kosher food." Yes, indeed we did. I suppose I didn't really need all that food anyway, and I have for sure improved on my cravings for non-kosher food. I've moved up from pining for Chick-Fil-A and Domino's to catered pseudo-kosher food.

As a newly observant Jew, I was also beginning to wonder whether the end justified the means. At times, I would hear of an Orthodox Jew who was so strict on his kashrut, yet lacking in good behavior, integrity or honest business practices. It took time until I learned that even Orthodox Jews are people too and 613 commandments are a lot for anyone person to master. Yet, there's an assumption, sometimes, that if you're Orthodox, or even attend an Orthodox shul, that you've mastered all 613 commandments. New flash: some of us are still working on the top ten. But, we *are* working on them.

Anyway, I remember my phone call to a major kashrut organization when I found bugs in one of their supervised boxes of matza meal. The head of this organization asked me what the problem was. I explained that I found bugs in my matza meal. What planet was he on? Bugs are *not* kosher. He told me it wasn't his problem as the infestation occurred after it left his supervision and hung up the phone. Huh? Was he religious? Orthodox? I was confused. Looking back, I was probably just projecting my own frustrations on this man, well on the entire industry. It wasn't that I thought he was personally responsible, but surely he had to care. Where was the connection? How could he be in charge of kosher food and be so cold at the same time? I was learning.

I was not able to separate their intention toward observing these laws from the people... who were just people. This unconscious living amidst an observant or so-called religious lifestyle baffled me. In other words, the rituals do not make the human being and definitely do not make the Jew. They are tools that many lose themselves in, and many find themselves in. There was no magic ticket to life or God or to being Jewish for that matter; they were opportunities (often missed). If this was going to be my life, then perhaps I needed to find the good, the meaning, the authenticity in it.

I found myself wondering about my own intentions. Perhaps, those who were less observant to the naked eye were even more religious than their "dressed up" counterparts? A rabbi in our community suggested that one should not be insulted, for example, if someone cannot eat in their home. But, I often wondered about the intentions of the one refusing. Was it coming from a place of love and understanding? I soon learned to not worry about intentions of others. We had to get creative upon accepting invitations and upon giving them out.

And for myself, I had to keep the purpose of our community and the Jewish people in the forefront: creating a Kiddush Hashem (living our lives as a sanctification to God). It just wasn't so simple.

So, I dove deep down into myself, into learning and I found some really awesome teachers who understood the essence of living an observant lifestyle. I found that the rituals if done with intention, not the kashrut alone, had the potential of elevating the mundane. These rituals had the potential of making every moment a conscious experience. For example, we say a blessing before and after eating any food, and there are different ones for each type of food. These blessings really bring consciousness to eating as they cause one to think about the particular food. As I like to say, the before blessing is for "thinking" and the after blessing is for "thanking."

Baruch or Yum?

This past week I had the opportunity to visit with some friends from our early-married years. During our mid twenties my aunt and uncle introduced us to a macrobiotic group, and we attended many potluck dinners together. I learned a lot....about brown rice, twig tea, seaweed and ying and yang. I recently caught up with two of my recovering-macrobiotic friends. As we were talking about food and macrobiotics and sharing stories, we began to discuss saying prayers before a meal. They inquired from me about what sort of prayer I said. So, I explained to them the different prayers. I explained that the word "baruch" has the same root as a "spring" (of water) and that we are not "blessing" God (after all, God does not need our blessings), but that we are recognizing the source of our food in detail (from a tree, the ground, grain, etc.) and ultimately from God. We are giving "attention" to the meal or food, as well as having "intention" toward eating. Both this attention and intention elevate the physical act of eating into a more spiritual act.

They found this all very interesting in a "Okay, we'll just move on from that" sort of way and said that they too had a prayer that they say before eating. I asked about it. They said that they took the "Ohm" from meditation and changed it to a "Yummmm." So, before they eat, they hold hands and say a loud, clear, energetic "Yum." I actually found their yum to be quite amazing and full of intention and attention. I have witnessed many "brachot" (blessings) with meaning and those that are void of any meaning or attention at all. If you say a blessing regularly, it is easy for it to become mundane. I know for myself, there are times I do them out of habit, but without thought. I was thinking that perhaps many of us could do with a good "Yum." It may not be very Jewish, but it is simple, to the point and heartfelt. I prefer our own blessings, but I may just add a personal "Yum" from now on. Well, here's to however you choose to show gratitude for your food: "Baruch" or "Yummmm." Enjoy!

I would often ask a religious authority why keeping Kosher does not equal eating healthfully or with a consciousness for the earth or body. I mean, how can we be allowed to ingest something like pareve ice cream? It's not food. It has twenty-three ingredients. It's a science experiment. The longer I live as an Orthodox Jew, the more like-minded people I have found who actually agree with me. But, in my early days I was told that although eating kosher can be healthful, it is a spiritual diet and not a physical one. To this day, I struggle with that. I do not think you can truly be a spiritual Jew without elevating the physical.

Once again, this just all came back to an intact hard drive or as I like to say, learning to be a human being first and then an Orthodox Jew. We cannot separate ourselves from what is going on around us or inside of us and be spiritual. We cannot eat well if others are starving or our food's ingredients look more like a science experiment than food. We can, however, put on the right clothing, cover our hair, adhere to the detail for every law and ritual and still not have the right intentions. That is every one of our struggles: to do what we need to do with a whole heart, for the sake of heaven and with integrity. Sometimes I found myself walking a fine line.

As I mentioned, we were fortunate enough to be invited over people's homes in our community for a meal. Although, I was jumping up and down with each invitation, my enthusiasm often put my husband into a high alert, as he was concerned with our eating at people's homes whose kashrut may not be "up to par." I wanted to go out, and he wanted to keep a close eye on what we ate. Since I did not want to delve into anyone else's personal or religious habits, I chose to accept invitations to those who lived in our community. In addition, I initially wasn't so fully observant myself. How does one really know when one is fully observant? If you keep every halacha but wear lipstick (no rubbing) on Shabbos, does that count? What if you secretly ripped off a loose thread from your skirt (no mending) on Shabbos? What if you keep every halacha but speak lashon hara (gossip)? Does that count?

Surely, I was in no position to assess anyone else's level of observance. So, I would accept the invitation and then, on occasion, my husband would say, "We can't eat there."

We would go back and forth as to why and I would end up having to call them up and back out of an invitation. This was *very* awkward. I usually won these heated discussions, as I pointed out that we were in a kiruv community (outreach) and we needed to reach out. That included accepting invitations. So, he came up with a requirement list: keeping kosher, being Shabbos observant and tovelling (purifying) your dishes. *Then*, sometimes he would agree to go. It was awkward for him too, as he would certainly find something that was "out of line."

Part of living in a community is spending time with people. Each time I went to a home, I connected with those families. Plus, honestly, I liked these people, well, and the break from cooking! I also found that people actually "raise the bar" when they have guests. We were sort of like a visit from the kashrut inspector. We by no means intended to come across as an authority toward our friends, but when you cover your hair or wear a black hat, sometimes you just do.

The problem between my husband and I was that I simply couldn't figure out where he would draw the line. It was confusing. It is not easy and I do not pass judgment on him for his adherence to the laws of kashrut. I suppose, we all draw the line somewhere. In fact, his adherence to those laws helped me along my own path. I often stood on the other side where people would not eat in my home as well. I'm sure it had something to do with my style of dress or my little dog. Yet, in the end, no matter where we eat, we never really know what goes on in the home, or restaurant for that matter; nor do we know the level of intention for those cooking or preparing the meal.

Is It Kosher Enough?

Recently, I offered my boys to have some friends over for a melava malka (festive meal right after Shabbos that extends the joy of Shabbos into the week) in lieu of a typical birthday party. Basically, it was a birthday party with less emphasis on the birthday and more emphasis on their friends and the melava malka. They were thrilled. Our plan was to serve pizza and cook out marshmallows. Seemed simple enough... Ha! They warned me that many of their friends have dietary restrictions (kosher dietary restrictions). I promised that no one would feel uncomfortable and we would accommodate everyone's needs. Anyway, for this party, that was hosting thirteen ten to eleven year old boys, I was told to make sure all the food was both Pas Yisroel and Cholov Yisroel. "Okay. I got it," I told them. "No Christmas cookies and no pig milk." "Mooooommm!!" they both chanted, "We're serious."

I promised to be careful. They checked on my purchases several times that week to be sure I would not embarrass them or their friends. Really? Me? Then came in one additional request. You also need to get Chabad meat. "What is Chabad meat?" I asked. "It's the Aaron's brand," my husband explained. Apparently, many years ago there was a Chabad vs. Satmar feud and now they don't eat each other's meat. In addition, there is Hasidish and non-Hasidish slaughtering. My husband only eats Hasidish. And, we wonder why we are all a bit loony? "Oh, and one more thing, Mom. Not all Pas Yisroel items are okay. You have to get the ones that are 'Yashan (old grain)." One of their friends only eats the non-Chabad meat and Pas Yisroel products with old grain. "Okie Dokie, " I replied. "Got it. Chabad meat for the Chabad friend. Hasidish meat for the non-Chabad friend. New grain for the pas Yisroel kids and old grain for the pas Yisroel Yashan friend. Anything else?" I inquired. "Nope, that should just about do it." So, off I went to the store stocking up on different milk and meat products and thanking God that none of these children were gluten intolerant or had a peanut allergy. Surely, God had bestowed me with blessings.

As I mentioned, if you want to be a part of an Orthodox community, you have to invite people over.....to EAT! There are always people to be invited (rich, poor, single, divorced, passing through town, friends, family, new to the community and so on), and if you have food, they will come. But, it was not always so simple for us (nor is it for anyone even if they make it look that way). There were those people who would not eat at our house because, who knows, I probably was not outwardly observant enough. Then, there were those who wouldn't eat because my husband was too religious (his Hassidic look can be a bit scary in Dunwoody, Georgia).

And, of course, there were those who were afraid of our dog ("ortho-dog-phobia" is a common disorder amongst Orthodox Jews from places like Baltimore, New Jersey and New York). Then we had to decide if we could have the Israelis with the Russians or the frum from birth with the modern Orthodox. There were also the soon-to-be-converts who we could not serve on holidays as the permission to cook on holidays is only permitted for the enjoyment of a Jew and not a non-Jew. This can all get very complicated, but interesting, as our warm community is very eclectic. It is so eclectic that just about anyone off the street can walk in (and they do) and feel comfortable. It is not that a red carpet will be laid out for you, but in our special shul in Dunwoody, Georgia, just about anyone is welcome.

Anyway, once people realized we were serving, they came! Then there was the question of what to feed them. Kosher food is expensive! I really wanted to go the tofu and rice route, but my husband vetoed that right away, and so I was left to buy "holy meat" for our carnivorous friends and learn how to cook the standard "soul food" such as chicken, cholent and kugel, and of course we adopted "Morah Dena's Mush" dish. It's basically a bunch of canned fruit thrown into a base of applesauce, but you'd think it was the dish of all dishes by the way people gobble it up. *Everyone* loves the mush, maybe, because it's the only food with color at her table. We serve it for dessert, but you can eat it anytime during the meal. From a culinary standpoint, it's an absolute necessity to balance out the sodium intake. Of course, my husband had to get the exact recipe, which I was asked not to deviate from or alter, but don't think I didn't try. This is how it's made:

- 1 Large Jar of applesauce
- 1 package of chopped frozen strawberries
- 1 can of pineapple (any form)
- 1 can mandarin oranges

- 1 can whole berry cranberry sauce

Then, mix it together in a large bowl and serve in small bowls or little cups. You can freeze the left over and use it again and again and again. And, then there's the Eggs and Onions dish. This dish offsets any benefit to your palette from the mush.

Eggs and Onions

My husband recently just returned from a rebbe sighting. He went to visit the Koidenover Rebbe. These trips inevitably end up with a new ritual or two or three. They keep me very pliable. This time he added a new dish: eggs and onions. Yep, my sentiments exactly. Apparently, the Rebbe asked my husband, "Does your wife prepare eggs and onions for you on Shabbos?" I later asked my husband, "Did you describe me to the Rebbe?" Not exactly.

It seems that the onions represent the manna that we ate in the desert. How? Well, the manna could taste like anything you wanted it to taste like: milkshakes, barbeque chicken, steak, Greek salad, you name it....except onions. It seems that is not good for nursing mothers to eat onions, so the manna would not even taste like them. To remember this, every Shabbos, we eat (myself included now) onions. I'm fortunate that mine are cooked. The eggs? Eggs are a sign of mourning and so we eat those to remember the loss of Moshe and David (the biblical ones) who died on Shabbos. This Hasidic custom has now infiltrated into my home and Shabbos table. Now, I can't just serve these eggs as a side dish; they need their own special attention. My husband wanted them as their own course.

And, this is where I revolted. There are simply too many courses already: wine, challah, fish, main, dessert. Green Peace is going to come after me if I add any more paper goods to my meal, and as much as I try to use real dishes, I don't have enough for five courses. He acquiesced and is allowing me to add the eggs and onions to the fishplate. Fish needs friends. Ah...the sweetness of a little victory. Now, keep in mind that my husband took full responsibility for preparing our Shabbos eggs and onions, bless his heart, and prepared them ahead of time (you too might want to prepare this dish ahead of time as otherwise there are about thirty-seven rules (really) for preparing it on Shabbos). He was so focused on his new little dish (I was out of town and not able to help with his first attempt at "onion bulb meets chicken bi-product"), that he almost served the main chicken dish raw neglecting to give it his full attention. Now, the chicken is insulted! "Oi vey iz mir," as my Buby used to say. Anyway, for the wannabe Hasid out there, here's a recipe that will keep your thoughts where they ought to be: focused on the manna:

- *1 cut up sweet onion*
- *3 eggs*
- *1 tsp. coconut oil*
- *1/2-teaspoon salt*
- *1 pinch black pepper*

Directions:

1. *Hard-boil the eggs. Shell them and halve them.*
2. *Chop up the onions*
3. *Add all the remaining ingredients and mix until everything is blended together. Do not turn this into a puree!*
4. *Turn into a dish and chill until needed.*
5. *Serve with challah, matzah, salad or whatever you fancy.*
6. *Eat.*
7. *Use mouthwash*

Mordechai realized that if he didn't step forward and do some of the cooking, we would lose all our friends. I realized that if I left all the cooking to him we would for sure lose them or at least be mortified from time to time, because no one was going for the eggs and onions. Whereas, I can create a killer soup, salad and vegetables, Mordechai can do the same with a cholent, kugel and meat dish. So, he became a huge help over the years and I slowly mastered a few great recipes myself. And, our friends, well....let's just say, those brave enough to spend time with us, came out none the worse, if not better from the experience. We even insulted some people by not inviting them often enough, "It's been a year since we last ate at your house." I mean a yid, his wife, their kids and their dog. It's almost enough for someone to blog about.

Serve it Their Way

When I was little, Burger King came up with this great marketing idea and a little tune that went "Hold the pickles. Hold the lettuce. Special orders don't upset us. All we ask is that you let us serve it your way." Well, I am not Burger King. Once, while I was serving up the dinner plates (Hasidic style), one guest let me know that he did not eat chicken, only red meat. Seems like he was on a "blood-type" diet, but forgot to tell me. That is like going to Pesach and not eating Matzah Balls (well actually non-Gebrochts Jews don't eat those, so that is not a great example, but you get the point). Anyway, that night I was serving chicken soup, won tons (with chicken that my husband made) and you guessed it, CHICKEN. I am fine if someone doesn't eat meat, etc., but in this case they asked if I had a replacement for the chicken. Okay, I know we're supposed to be like Abraham, being all welcoming and all, but after preparing twenty-three meals over the high holidays and trying to make sure I have soup, fish, salad, challah, wine, kugel, main dish, dessert, etc. for all these meals, I was not feeling up to the Burger King way, so I handed him some kugel and with a smile said, "I hope you enjoy it." In general, after being a guest and a host for many years now, I have learned the following:

- *If you absolutely cannot consume a certain type of food, please send your dietary restrictions ahead of time.*
- *Do offer to bring something. Grocery stores have aisles packed with kosher food. Oh, and that bottle of kosher white zinfandel that nobody wants....your host will probably re-gift it or use it for cooking.*
- *Please watch after your own children. Your host is not your baby sitter.*
- *Come to have fun, to learn, to engage, to share, but leave your issues at home. Your host is more than likely not a therapist and even if they are, it's Shabbos!*

Generally, I start preparing for the Shabbos on any given Tuesday when I head to the store. I use Wednesdays and Thursdays to cook for the Shabbos lunch meal and Friday for the Shabbos dinner meal. My friend, Kim, knows how to order really well and so she dials up a phenomenal meal any time she has guests. That can cost a pretty penny, so most of us cook. Our rebbetzin can be found any late Thursday evening at our local Kroger with a buggy so full that it nearly fills up her entire twelve-passenger van to get the groceries home. She then cooks until the wee hours of the night and into the morning (usually ½ asleep). The result is a beautiful Shabbos meal for around forty people with some very well-done food. And, although no one claims to come for the food, we really like it, and generally there is nothing left on the table by the end of the Shabbos. Over the years, Mordechai and I have served some horribly burnt food. One time my husband decided to "crock-pot" meatballs. They were so over-cooked you could have used them as golf balls. There was also the time our grill caught on fire and we tried to save the scorched chicken. We thought no one would notice. They did.

Our People

"To love someone is the deepest thing in the world, but you can't prove it. You can't put your finger on it, but it's the most real thing in the world. God is the most, utmost real thing in the world, and you can't see Him, but after you don't see Him, you see Him. Then you can see Him everywhere, in every flower, in every cloud, in every little stone, in every candle."
Rabbi Shlomo Carlebach

My Dog for Two Rabbis

Last Shabbos I was out of town. I arranged for my husband, daughter and twin boys to have their Shabbos meals with friends. So, off I go to Indianapolis (home of one kosher bakery) with my provisions on hand, happy that my family was left to enjoy Shabbos in the company of good people. Not too far into my trip, I get a call from my husband explaining that he had been asked to host two Hasidic rabbis and was shipping my dog off to Camp Cuddle Care (aka: doggie overnight care). Since I was several hundred miles away, hearing the determination in his voice and my thoughts focused on the convention I was attending, I wished him well (and said a silent prayer for my daughter who would be put to the test with two extra, long-bearded rabbis in the house). It was only after I was going to bed Erev Shabbos, that I began to process that my little dog had been traded out for two rabbis. Seriously?? She was worth at least ten! She is super sweet, soft and cuddly and would never turn down the chesed (loving kindness) of welcoming a stranger into our home. I mean how can anyone not fall in love?

SINCE WHEN DID RABBIS BECOME
MAN'S BEST FRIEND?

Well, it seems as if the rabbis were a huge hit with my boys, while my husband managed to cook, prepare and clean up from two major Shabbos meals (he is very capable no doubt) and a Melava Malka; and my dog had a blast at Camp Cuddle Care. She is just now, however, coming out of her depression from being "traded." It will take some time, but a good dose of chicken soup and challah should set her straight. Maybe my husband's right and she really is a dog. I kept thinking she's a reincarnated person, but my husband says it's not possible; as to be reincarnated as a dog is a punishment. However, after much thought, he has come to the conclusion that to be reincarnated as a dog in our house, is a reward.

Meanwhile, this past week, my boys managed to convince me to purchase a fish and a bird. My husband cried. Ah, divine retribution at its best.

My husband is known as Mike to the people he works with, Michael to people he grew up with and Mordechai to people who know him now. But no matter how people have known him, he is loved, respected and, well, usually, the center of the party. He loves people and people love him. Mordechai is often asked a plethora of questions depending on the audience. "So what kind of Hasid are you? Did you grow up Hasidic? How many Hasidim are there in Atlanta? How did you become Hasidic?" He loves to explain it to an interested crowd, but nothing makes him happier than hanging with other Hasidim. He refers to them as "My People." He's not too picky about his flavor of Hasid, although last I heard we were Koidenover Hasidim. Although he identifies with the Slonim Hasidim, he has more of a relationship with the Koidenover Rebbe in Benei Brak. Either way, he loves to meet, read and "tish" with just about anyone strolling the streets in a long black coat, black furry hat and donning a plethora of religious garb.

Eenie Meenie Minie rebbe

The other night my husband told me he was soon going to pick one of two rebbes (Hasidic rabbis) to follow. There are many of them, but he has two that he has been following for a while. It seems that the one he has been following is a bit harder to connect with and the other is more available. Being that I will probably never encounter either one, I have to rely on my husband's choosing, which WILL directly affect my life. I put a vote in to find a "happy" one and maybe one who wears a tie, as I'd really like to add some color back to my husband's wardrobe. Apparently, you can swap out rebbes without too much difficulty. Anyway, I asked him to compare them for me so I could understand what our choices were. He explained that one of them uses a smooth knife to cut the challah and the other uses a serrated knife. He also said that one uses the word "gefen when reciting the Kiddush and the other uses "gafen (both meaning fruit of the vine)." In addition, he explained that one eats fish with his fingers and one eats fish with a fork.

He then went quiet.

I said, "So?? That's it?! We're choosing a rebbe based on his knife preference, pronunciation of a word and finger or fork usage?" Well, it seems obvious to me. I say we go with the serrated-knife-rebbe as the serrated knife doesn't destroy the challah, but cuts it nicely. I have a friend who's also married to a Hasid, and he also tried to pull the knife stunt on her. He showed up one week with a smooth knife that nearly mutilated her beautiful challahs. She stood firm and warned him that if he wanted to continue eating the challah, he had to put away the smooth knife.

I told my husband that I was sure there were a few more points that he was forgetting to fill me in on. He smiled and said, "Of course." To which I asked him if he wouldn't mind making me a poster board with our new customs once he has figured out which rebbe is our man. He smiled. So my future is "up in the air," until further notice. Please stay tuned. I'm sure I will have a lot to fill you in on.

So what is a rebbe? He is different than a rabbi. Although, I know a few rabbi's who could qualify for rebbes too. A rabbi answers questions; a rebbe answers people. A rabbi hears what you say with your mouth; a rebbe hears what you are saying with your soul. A rebbe is a spiritual teacher, an advisor, a leader and generally a very righteous man.

Just in case you might be interested, Koidenov is a Hasidic dynasty that was founded by Rabbi Shlomo Chaim Perlow in

1833. Its present day city is Dzyarzhynsk, Belarus. Koidanov was the smallest of the three Lithuanian Hasidic dynasties, the others being Slonim and Karlin-Stolin. At the start of World War II, its centers of influence were in the regions of Koidanov and Minsk. After its rebbes and most of its Hasidim were murdered in the Holocaust, the dynasty was re-established in 1948 in Tel Aviv, where it thrives to this day. Under Rebbe Yaakov Tzvi Meir Ehrlich's direction, the Koidanover dynasty maintains synagogues in Tel Aviv and Bnei Brak and a yeshiva, in addition to chesed projects. The Rebbe is heavily involved in kiruv (outreach). His beis midrash, located in Dizengoff Square, serves as an outreach center where weekly lectures and a Friday-night Oneg Shabbat attract many secular Jews and guide them towards religious observance. Rebbe Yaakov Tzvi Meir is well known as an inspiring speaker and educator of youth.[1]

Rebbe Visit

The Rebbe came to town. My husband was on an all time high. He loves Hasidis, and it is a gift for him to have a rebbe nearby. My husband offered for me to have a personal visit with the Rebbe, but I declined, not because I don't think his blessing would be good, but because well....I'm just not so comfortable around the Rebbe. I did enjoy his visit to our community and especially his egg story. This is how it goes.

A newly married couple was discussing their relationship and the man told his new wife that although he didn't want to keep any secrets from her, she was not to go into his drawer. She promised. For twenty years she did not go in the drawer. But, one evening he was really late and her curiosity got the best of her. So, she opened the drawer. What did she find? $100,000 and five eggs. When her husband came home, she asked, "I'm sorry I went in your drawer. I understand the $100,000 as I like *to spend a lot, so I'm sure you put some money aside; but why the five eggs?" He replied, "I put an egg in the drawer each time we had an argument instead of fighting." She replied, "Wow! Only five eggs in twenty years. That is amazing," to which he replied, "Well every time I had a dozen, I sold them."*

Now thinking that this rebbe was entertaining, at the least, I ran home and told our daughter, that she could go get a blessing. She looked right at me and said, "But what do I ask for?" I replied, "Whatever you'd like." Carmelle, age fifteen at the time, ran up to our synagogue and waited patiently in line to see the Rebbe. As she entered, he asked her what blessing she would like, to which she replied, "I'd like to be a famous actress." He looked at her with such sincerity and asked, "What is this 'actress'. You will have to explain it to me."

The first time I heard Mordechai use the phrase "my people," I felt insulted and left out. Why did he need his own group of people? What was wrong with having his own family or community being "his people?" Aren't *they* our people? It felt like I had given up my close ties with *my people*: holidays and certain gatherings with my immediate family, Camp Barney, Or Ve Shalom and Conservative Judaism for Orthodoxy and the Ariel people, and now he had a whole new group of people that I couldn't even relate to. Would he ever really find "his people?" Hasidim were more like imaginary people to me and to our children. It's not that we never met them, but for the most part they were people we saw on a video, in a magazine, in a book and in photos that were multiplying across our mantle. They were virtual people, and to be honest, they didn't look all too friendly. I wasn't getting a warm fuzzy, no happy place. And, to top it off, there were no women to be seen. I mean, there were women, but they were in their houses, with their children, running their lives. There are no groups of Hasidic women in photos, dancing on computers, in Atlanta or at Ariel. Plus, I wasn't dressed for the part. In Genesis (44:30) it says, "His soul is bound up with his soul." Rebbe Nachman of Breslev in the Likutei Moharan (I,135) explains that when a person attains great love for the tzaddik (righteous person), he is bound to the tzaddik's soul. I was feeling left out of this soul binding experience. I wanted my husband binding with my soul, not a rebbe's soul.

Mordechai would sometimes say to me, "I want to take you to visit a Hasidic community, but we have to cover you up." That offended me, rightfully so. But, he was right in one respect. You can't go into those communities and appear disrespectful to their way of life. I'm not saying that they shouldn't look beyond the surface, but I understand how hard that might be given their culture. I like people who stand out, but not everyone does. Mordechai would often tell me, "We're into "same," not "different." Problem was, I was into "different," not "same." I just didn't understand why he needed his own group of people when he had me, our family and Ariel. I also didn't understand asking the Rebbe if you wanted to eat a certain dish or include a prayer or song to sing. I often felt as if my husband was choosing the Rebbe over me or rather over himself.

There is a beautiful prayer (the Song of Ascents) that is sung before the Birchat Hamazon on festivals and the Sabbath. Many people do not sing the last paragraph, but it is a beautiful praise of God. I wanted to sing it, not solo, but for us as a family to include it. Mordechai would not do so, without the approval of the Rebbe. I didn't understand what the Rebbe had to do with our family's choice of praise. And, although my boys looked Hasidic, they are just regular kids, with payos (side locks), who like Harry Potter and video games. My daughter one day said to me, "Mom, I think to be a Hasidic rebbe you only need to do two things: grow a really long beard and don't look at women." From her perspective, this was all she saw.

The Rebbe Came to Town

This past Shabbos, we packed up the car and headed across town to be with the Rebbe. My daughter had already met him at her school and gave him a big thumbs up as "he actually looked at me." This is a step in the right direction if you want to get the approval of a teen-aged girl, or anyone for that matter. I did notice that he had very kind, soft, blue eyes, and he said something nice to me (not exactly sure, but I think it was along the lines that I should have a long happy marriage to which I replied "amen"). It pretty much doesn't matter what a rebbe says to you. The correct reply is always "amen."

The other day my boys were asking my husband about all the different rebbes as they are quite fascinated with them (I tend to get them all confused) and he began to list them all off. I was actually surprised by how many there are and how many my husband knows. I mean, I've been living with the man for twenty-five years! Just to name a few....there's the
Slonimer Rebbe
Koidenover Rebbe
Bobover Rebbe
Skverer Rebbe
Kaalover Rebbe
Belzer Rebbe
Boyaner Rebbe
Munkatcher Rebbe
Ger Rebbe
Viznitzer Rebbe
Skulener Rebbe
Bostoner Rebbe
Rimanover Rebbe
Nikolsburger Rebbe
Satmar Rebbe
Burshtein Rebbe
And, just a few more....

They get their names from the towns in which they originated (not the most creative bunch but then again they don't have to worry about trademark infringement). I'm not sure what happens, though, if two pop up out of the same town. Anyway, my husband began to explain that when he was in NY, he saw the Munkatcher Rebbe walking down the street one night and how his face was all aglow. He described it as just being so bright, almost like a light bulb in the distance. Well, I thought that was pretty cool (really seeing someone whose face lights up) and so I said, "Well isn't that how he got his name, the Moon Catcher?" My husband and kids nearly fell out of their chairs with hysterical laughter. Sad thing was, I wasn't even trying to be funny. And, that in a nutshell clearly explains why I am not going to be "tishing" with the Rebbe.

Over time, I came to realize that much of my dislike toward these "men in black" was a result of my own insecurities and perhaps just a twinge of Mordechai's OOD (Obsessive Orthodox Disorder). We all have groups we relate to in one way or another. We have our work friends, our neighborhood friends and so on. We all bring groups of people into our marriages, and I had not lost any of my people. There were my people, his people and now our people. It's just that his most recent "people" were just a bit more extreme and different, in every way imaginable. Yet, they were also joyous, at least they seem to be. Mordechai would often show me a video or photo of a few hundred Hasidic men and ask me, "Aren't they so cool?" I wanted to see the "coolness," but I had a hard time relating. So, one day I asked him, "If I showed you 500 women dancing together would you think it was cool?" To which, he replied, "Of course!" Then again, I suppose he would.

Their dress was so different too. I had finally integrated into wearing an observant dress code, and, yet, his people considered my dress disrespectful. I remember one time a

Hasidic rabbi came to our home for dinner. This was a big deal, and I was nervous. As I mentioned, Hasidic men wear a long black coat, a bekesha. They don't take it off. I didn't realize at the time, but a bekesha is not a coat, it's their holy garb, their "spirit wear." I heard them coming to the door. I made sure everything was ready, and I opened the door to greet them and said, "Can I take your coat?" Mordechai's face went white. He realized right then that I was way out of my league. Mordechai loved the discomfort that this experience brought to our home. I, however, had no need to feel uncomfortable. I was not all too happy being the sacrifice for his much needed spiritual lift. I think, perhaps, we've all done that at times, sacrificing a loved one for our own needs.

Rabbis On The Wall

I've been married for twenty-six years, and rebbes have popped up on our walls. My husband would put them up and I would take them down. Some rabbis are alive, some are dead, none are smiling and well....none are related to us. Yet my sweet husband is so happy bringing them into our home and hanging them in various spots throughout our house. They appear to be multiplying as my resistance to them has diminished. If you can imagine the Hogwarts School of Magic with all the wizard photos, well just switch those out for rabbi photos. Our sukkah displays an entire two and a bit walls of rabbis and as I look at them I wonder what their wives were like. Who were these women who devoted their entire lives to these men? Did their husbands drive them crazy? Probably. Wouldn't you like to be a fly on the wall in one of their sukkahs?

At any rate, there they are watching me go in and out my daily routines and I hope sending us blessings. Recently I have taken up drawing portraits of the rebbes. Funny enough, I find it therapeutic. There is something mysterious about each one and I find it calming to put their essence onto a canvas. One day a collector (for charity) came to our house and was outraged that my drawing of one of the rebbes had lips that were too red (Hey, I'm no Picasso). My husband tried to explain to him that his wife was just a bit "out of the box" and truly meant no disrespect. I think perhaps I should have been highly insulted, but it only made me laugh. By the way, the rebbe drawing has moved upstairs. My boys love the drawing, and they think the artist rocks!

Over the years my attitude toward these gentle giants has changed. I was fortunate enough to meet some of the most loving, kind Hasidic rebbes including Shlomo Carlebach and most recently rabbi Lazer Brody and the Koidenover Rebbe himself...Well, I met his wife, but he smiled at me from a distance and even greeted me. I was told this was a "big deal." I even went tish hopping (visiting various rebbe's tables through wee hours of the night). My daughter and I renamed it "t-shopping," as it was somewhat like hopping from store to store in a mall, just no mall and no stores. We escalated hundreds of stairs to women's sections and peered down at a lot of men swaying near their rebbe, who sat and ate and mumbled something we couldn't hear or understand. But, I loved the experience and got an amazing stair-climbing workout. It is hard not to sense the joy and love that radiates from certain Hasidim. Shlomo Carlebach transformed thousands of Jewish lives from the sixties to the eighties with his music and loving nature. You can't help but feel joy and love that radiates from Rabbi Brody's warm smile and teachings on emunah (faith). Just a mere few minutes with people such as those is enough to make you want to be....a Hasid.

Holy rebbes

My husband and boys are heading across town this Shabbos, yes, again, to see a rebbe. I am staying back with our dog. Now don't go getting your feminist feathers all ruffled. Even though that might come off as a bit 'third world,' it is my choice. His visit will be like a religious men's club brouhaha. In addition, each rebbe seems to travel with an entourage and have certain "requirements" (what he can eat, when he eats, what he drinks)....they all seem a bit "tipsy"... I suppose they need a little "boost" to stay in their connected frame of consciousness. Anyway, the rebbe holds a "tish." It's like a bunch of guys watching the football game with beer, except there's no game and no beer. There is Torah and schnapps, singing and dancing. Instead of passing the bowl of popcorn around, for example, they might pass the Rebbe's challah or soup around (that right there would keep me away). It seems like anything the Rebbe touches can be holy. At any rate, should you ever get to attend a tish, go! There are great discussions, and it can be a spiritual lift (if you can understand the rebbe as not all of them speak in English). Meanwhile, I will be getting a little R&R...with my dachshund. I'll pass my challah to her, and she will gobble it up. Makes me feel like her rebbe.

It has taken me a long time to understand Mordechai's yearning toward Hasidim and Hasidus. He likes to point out that his great-great grandfather was a Hasid. From the people whom I've met in his family and extended family, it is hard to imagine. Yet, he has slowly injected bits and pieces of Hasidis into our family, sometimes forcefully and sometimes gently. Sometimes it fits nicely into our lifestyle and daily routines and well, sometimes, it just doesn't. Sometimes I find myself in a dichotomy that is just mind blowing.

Sex Change

Recently my husband and I decided we needed to update some of our legal documents. We are both very busy and decided to ask the lawyer who had drafted the original ones if he could update them. My husband said he would take care of this and make an appointment for us to sign the documents. As he was notifying me that he had located the lawyer and scheduled the appointment, he said, "And, oh, by the way, he is not a he anymore. He had a sex change." "Really?" I replied. "Yes, Samuel is now Samantha. But, he, I mean, she is a really good lawyer. He did offer to have our documents sent to a different lawyer if we're not comfortable, but I just thought this would be quick and easy." Well, I'm thinking, this should be interesting. It's not often in my Orthodox world that I find myself with those who have had a sex change. This has added some excitement to my day.

The day of our appointment comes. My husband is in a quandary. Since, according to halacha, a man does not shake a woman's hand, the question is whether my husband should shake her (Samantha's aka: Samuel's) hand. I shrugged my shoulders, as I was stupefied.

This was just getting better by the moment.

Well, off we go to our liberal lawyer meeting. Samantha extends her hand to my husband and, lo and behold, he shakes it. It really is not my husband's style to embarrass anyone in these circumstances. There is a loophole for that.

I get to meet Samantha, and, truth be told, I didn't really remember Sam. It's hard not to notice that something is "different." I find it hard to concentrate on the legal talk as I'm so distracted by the idea of someone changing their sex; and, I really like her earrings. I'm wondering where she got them. I can't stop staring. I'm wondering which body parts are real. I find myself almost giddy, and on the verge of a "silly" panic attic from thinking of the irony of the situation I'm in. I mean I'm sitting between two people who could not be more different in every aspect imaginable and we're just having a normal conversation. I'm having a hard time containing myself without physically slapping myself, and, so, I *excuse myself to the restroom to tell myself to "hold it together." I'm wishing I had some Xanax before I go back, and I don't even take Xanax. Maybe I should start... like, right now.*

I go back to the meeting. Samantha is very nice and intriguing to say the least. My husband informs her that we are celebrating our twenty-fifth anniversary. I'm thinking, "Oh...let's NOT talk about marriage." But, she then informs us that she is married and she is celebrating her twenty-seventh anniversary. Now, I'm really interested. "To whom?" I ask, before my husband slaps me under the table. Well...I'm just curious. She is celebrating with her wife of twenty-seven years. Seems like they take the commitment thing really seriously. His wife stayed with him during the sex change, and they are still married! It is just hard to digest, even for me. I guess I'm not as liberal as I thought I was. But, even so, my heart goes out to those who struggle with their sexual orientation. It cannot be easy. But, then again, we all have our struggles.

Well, there we are: me, my Hasidic husband and this woman or man (I'm still not so sure) just having a "normal" conversation. I know God was having a hay day with me. When I get to the next world, my life movie is for sure going to have a review of this office visit, including my intermission break to the restroom.

Not too long ago, Mordechai had invited some of our Ariel friends as well as some Hasidic rabbis to our home for a tish. He alerted me that he needed to kasher our oven, as these rabbis were "Cholov Yisroel." He told me that Hasidim are all Cholov Yisroel, and so they assume we are too, to which I replied, "Why do they think we are?" He rolled his eyes at me because, truthfully, he would also be Cholov Yisroel if I hadn't put my foot down. It's just not so easy being Cholov Yisroel in Atlanta, Georgia. Maybe it's not so hard, but not so easy either.

But, this is our journey: trying to learn, grow and accommodate. Maybe, that is the point. Not getting comfortable. But, that is who we are, and I am, well, for better or ....for better...married to a....yid, a Hasidic yid.

Blood Relatives

It would be hard for me to pass up telling you about the rest of "our people." They are our extended families. Like most families, each person comes with his or her own story. We have family members from all walks of faith. I'm a 100% sure that we give them plenty to talk about. The fact that they have stuck by us, in spite of our becoming observant, religious and Hasidic shows amazing character, if not tolerance, on their part. Both sides of our families have embraced us, loved us, made accommodations for us and celebrated with us. That actually sometimes made it hard for us in a different way. As observing Jews, sometimes we could not participate with them and we wanted to. But, we were on a journey, and the fact that they were always cheering us on, albeit sometimes understandably avoiding us, was in my opinion, divine. I'm sure they had conversations like, "The Dannemans invited us over. Is there anywhere else we could go to for Pesach Seder?" But, we all laugh about it. They have even gone so far as to buy us our own cardboard-kosher-frozen pizza while they ate Domino's. Mordechai's brother even bought us our own grille. Either way, we appreciate them encouraging us to make a scene at their homes, and as I have always taught my children so well, "Family comes first. You suffer for family." And, suffer we all do, together, but we'd have it no other way.

Chinese New Year

So... our extended family is heading out to their traditional Chinese dinner this year. They nearly forfeited this outing to go to a kosher restaurant. I know! Can you believe it? That is a step closer than the past years when it wasn't even a thought. My brother in particular loves restaurants. He is forever taking photos of each dinner plate he's served from anywhere in the world and posting them on Facebook. This either means he's obsessed or my sister-in-law doesn't do much cooking. Anyway, I understand budgets, and I don't expect them to eat at the one or two kosher restaurants on my behalf, although they do often enough. I was even surprised by the consideration! I would have offered kosher Chinese take-out food at home, but they have a tradition and the take-out is closed. So, they will continue on with their tradition of chicken chow mein, sizzling rice soup and beef and broccoli on Christmas Day at the Lucky Key. The Chinese people love the Jews and they love Christmas Day when Jews frequent their restaurants. The movie theaters love us too. My extended family will sit all huddled together laughing, eating and having a wonderful time. My boys and I will join them for the movie. We will pass up the Lucky Key. This is the sacrifice I make year after year with more than just this occasion.

I actually find peace in all of this, though. As hard as this is for me to understand, there is a grand plan playing out, whether it personally benefits me or not. I don't claim to understand it, nor do the Chinese restaurant owners. But, somehow this is all going to work itself out. Either our next generation of Jews are all going to become very comfortable with the Chinese and a variety of other traditions that land in their lap, we are all going to wake up and realize that keeping kosher outweighs eating Chinese, or someone really smart is going to open a great sit-down, kosher Chinese restaurant and offer "Chinese and a Movie" on Christmas Day. I'm putting my reservation in now!

Our Community

It was Congregation Ariel that taught me, taught us, about community. Sometimes it was hard to tell whether we were part of a synagogue or a rehab center. I think just by its nature, Orthodoxy attracts people with a "background." The Torah and an Orthodox lifestyle offer a firm footing to someone who may be at the bottom of their rope. I'm not suggesting that it only serves those who have hit bottom, but it can for sure be attractive to them. And, we all support each other. Spending so many days together (weekdays, Shabbos, holidays), especially the three-day-marathon-holidays without phone, car, computer or a shower, can create quite a bonding experience that people outside cannot quite understand or tolerate for that matter. A week after we showed up at Ariel for the first time, we were invited to stay for lunch. It was there that I first learned about removing bugs from strawberries. Maybe it was the nervousness from our rebbetzin, when I offered to help rinse the strawberries. Was she worried that my hands were not clean? We had never worried so much about fruit: just rinse and eat. It's funny how that stuck with me.

But, I also saw something different. It was the rabbi's older daughters, twelve and thirteen at the time, who struck a chord in me. They had self-esteem, but it didn't come from a focus *on* them. It seemed to be coming *from* them. They seemed to feel as if they had something to offer, something of value that was outside of their physical selves, talents or emotions. This worthiness extended outside of our rabbi's family, outside of our synagogue and permeated throughout our community. Sometimes it even showed up at our front door.

The UPS Man Bringeth and the rabbi (Schnorer) Taketh Away

174

As members of a religious community, we are frequented by "visitors." They have needs. Financial ones. Over the years we have opened our door hundreds of times and sometimes at most inconvenient times, but we welcome the mitzvah, well, honestly we try to. My husband and I have our favorite tzedakah (charitable organizations) that we feel blessed to give money to each year. Some of them are larger, and I donate online, and others visit our door annually through a collector. Between regular collectors and UPS (I work out of my home and order a bit online), our bell rings several times a day. Thank God for UPS. About eleven years ago, when I found myself housebound after having twins, I began to order online...everything. I rarely go to a store anymore. So, the UPS man was a frequent visitor. We love his visits. Even my husband enjoys seeing him stop at our house. When my husband asks if he gets tired of visiting us, the UPS man says "No. Your wife is good job security." We really should get to know him better and offer him some food and drink, but he's so fast that he is in and out of sight like a bolt of lightning.

As I mentioned, in addition to the UPS man, we are also frequented by rabbi's collecting charity (tzedakah). Some of them are just so cute and happy. They come with a letter that is approved by our local rabbi so we know they are collecting for a legitimate tzedakah. So, when the doorbell rings, we run to see whether it is the UPS man or a Tzedekah man. Yet lately, it is not the UPS man and not a tzedakah man. It is a "shnorer" man. You see whereas the Lord giveth and the Lord taketh away, the UPS man bringeth and the shnorer taketh away.

A shnorer is not a tzedakah man. A shnorer is a story man. He makes up stories in order to collect money. He knows how to pull your guilt strings and then you feel like you were schnooked, which totally negates any good will. So, I've come up with a few tips for handling the Shnorer

Man (these tips should not be used on legitimate collectors):

1. Get a large dog. Most of them think they are horses or wild beasts and will avoid your house. We have a little dachshund, so it is not as effective, but works when we tell them she's an overgrown rat.
2. Have a bowl of candy ready and say "Trick or Treat."
3. Give them a $1.00 and a big hug and say "Thank you for opportunity to do a mitzvah!"
4. Tell them you are so happy that they stopped by because you are collecting for your local Orthodox school and ask them if they can donate.
5. Offer them a job
6. Tell them your neighbor (the one you don't like) is giving out double today, but the offer runs out in five minutes.
7. Have your young child (the one throwing the tantrum) answer the door.
8. Well, if you have a heart, ignore numbers 1-7 and go ahead and give them. Give freely and openly. Surely, you are blessed if you are able to give.

Sofer Situations

My husband is a sofer. A sofer is a scribe that hand writes Torah scrolls and the parchments in tefillin and mezuzot. He is not just any sofer; he is an outstanding sofer. He is meticulous, artistic and heartfelt. He almost never turns down an opportunity to fix a Torah. He does not question the audience but takes the opportunity to educate them. On many occasions he gets called from Jews of "many flavors" (as he kindly puts it) to fix their "not-so-kosher" Torah or to purchase a new one. We are both always touched by the sincerity of those bringing their precious Torah into our homes. They are generally wrapped and handled with care. We are never too *surprised and yet surprised enough by what comes into our home. This past week we were presented a Torah wrapped in a purple sleeping bag with a pink flower on it. My husband treated that Torah with the exact same intentions as he would one found buried under the Temple in Jerusalem. He inspected it, corrected it and returned it to its owner wrapped in its purple bag with the pink flower. Because, you see, it is what's on the inside that matters. This lesson we have learned and we learn each and every day. All in a day's work.*

The people at Congregation Ariel are our family. When we first came to Ariel it was more like a little steibel (little room). It is now a flourishing community. Everyone who comes to Ariel has a story... and I mean everyone. We have observant members, non-observing members, converts, non-Jews, Israelis, Russians, lost souls, suffering souls, religious ones and of course, a couple of furry hats: Hasidim. The people at Ariel love us, and the feeling is mutual. They love us in spite of our differences and because of them. I never feel judged at Ariel. I have a special connection with the women who are like sisters, and it is to them, for sure, that I owe so much of my personal growth. It is their shoulders that I so frequently lean on or pull myself up on when I need a lift. They offer me an ear, counseling, support and encouragement. We are always feeding each other too. We feed each other when we're sick, when there's a simcha (joyous occasion), anytime we sit down and just about anywhere for any reason. They are role models for me. Amongst all these people are our amazing rabbis (my husband included), led by Rabbi Binyomin Friedman, who teach us, push us (well, sometimes they shove us) and encourage us to learn and grow. One concept that permeates this community is *gratitude*. With all the ups and downs, no matter the circumstance, what I always see are people showing gratitude: toward each other, toward life and mostly toward God. The phrase "Baruch Hashem (Thank God)" rolls off their tongues on a regular basis. And, from that gratitude I see blessings. It is as if it opens up a receptor for goodness in their life. So, these are "our people." I am committed to them and to Ariel's mission to "connect, share and grow." *Our people* teach us so much, shower us with love and make us laugh; and, well, sometimes we just do the same for them.

The 11th Commandment: Thou Shalt Not Re-Gift

It is customary in our community, although not necessary, to bring a small token or gift to someone's home when they have invited you for a Shabbos meal. It is fine, of course, if you show up without a gift, but a small gift is a way of showing your appreciation. This is not unique to Orthodox Jews by any means. Sometimes I stop by a local farmers market and send over fresh produce, or during planting season, I might provide some of my own homegrown vegetables. Sometimes I might send over a dessert, some candy, flowers or a bottle of wine (the "I didn't really have time to think of you, so just grabbed this off the shelf gift). I've even been known to welcome a new family with a huge jar of pickles.

Anyway, after my mother-in-law's unfortunate passing, we had several packaged cakes sitting on our counter from people who had brought us food during the Shiva. The Shabbos after shiva, we were invited out for two Shabbos meals: Friday night dinner and Shabbos day (lunch, or the second meal). Both families live on the same street. I packed up some home grown banana peppers for each family, stopped by and picked them both up some farm-fresh tomatoes and then noticed the two cakes. I decided I would re-gift these, as we would not be eating them. I dropped off the items at the first house and then headed to the second house. I immediately noticed a look of recognition in the face of my soon-to-be host. I then realized I had re-gifted the very cake that I later found out she had brought to us from New York from a special Hasidic bakery. Gulp. I retracted my cake offering to take it back home, as "I didn't realize it was all the way from NY!" I immediately started a silent vidui (confession) promising to never re-gift again, when I noticed the son of the first family running across the front yard and into the home where I was now standing feeling remorseful. He had in his hand the cake that I had just dropped off at his house and was re-gifting my re-gifted cake to the same family from whom I was taking back the second re-gifted cake. I silently began hitting my chest even harder knowing that my first re-gifted cake had been rejected and was now sitting on the counter of the woman whom I had just retracted my second re-gifted cake. I then decided not only would I never re-gift, but also I would do an extra special vidui come Yom Kippur.

I still need to drop off a baby gift to two families. I have a few baby toys that were never opened. Problem is, I don't remember who gave them to me. I think I'll give them some post-partum pickles.

1: Koidanov (Hasidic dynasty) - Wikipedia, the free encyclopedia. (n.d.). Retrieved from http://en.wikipedia.org/wiki/Koidanov_(Hasidic_dynasty)

For the LOVE of God

I am a tree
A witness to a place
Where God kissed the earth
And the power of His kiss
Makes roots to grow
And reach so deep
And trunks to form
And branches to extend
And leaves to grow

Flower to bloom
And fruit to bear
Each kiss creates
A tree not like
Any other
Its attributes unique
And the gift of the kiss
Keeps giving long after
It has touched this earth
The tree is then the giver
Of sight, shade, fruit,
Flower, wood
And even in its
Death, the kiss keeps
Giving...to the soil
That nourished it
..to future trees
...to the earth
....and back to heaven again

I had a roommate in college who, at the time, I thought was somewhat of a religious freak. She wore that name proudly. There is no doubt that I was living sub-spiritually in comparison. Whereas she had made a daily choice to live from her highest self, I didn't even know I had a highest self. I tried to loosen her up a bit, but to no avail. She would just smile and say something like, "Aw, Ilana, sorry I can't go to that party. I'm going to a bible study." Bible study? Really? She said a silent blessing over her food *every* time she ate, dressed conservatively and prayed *a lot*. I was always amazed *and* perplexed at how internally strong she was. She never deviated from her mission of "walking with God." Where the rest of us were easily influenced by culture, nature, emotions, boyfriends and by each other, she was not. She knew who she was and, at least from my perspective, her ultimate purpose here, in being a messenger of God.

She wasn't Jewish.

Looking back, now, as the token Jew in my class, I surely missed an opportunity. At the time, I only heard of non-Jewish people having "a relationship with God." I didn't know anyone who talked about God like she did. I thought Jewish people just celebrated holidays, sang songs, supported Israel and ate matzah ball soup. I went to Jewish day school and high school but never understood that the Torah was for me. I thought of it as an antiquated text. I thought the oral law was the "telephone game" gone bad. I thought rabbis just followed a bunch of rules because, well, they were rabbis. I figured they rocked back and forth a lot because they all had sensory integration disorders.

I have learned differently.

It used to be that when I would glance at religious people, I'd feel something strange. I was uncomfortable in my own skin. Sometimes I still am. Sometimes feel I have to make excuses for myself, for my kids, for Mordechai. I might struggle for just a moment, but I know why. It is hard to connect to my highest self when it's buried under a lot of "stuff." Whether I like it or not, my past is a part of me, and often a springboard toward a better me. One of my favorite authors and motivational speakers, Debbie Ford, O.B.M. wrote in *Why Good People Do Bad Things*, "Every fall from grace and self-destructive move is drenched in holiness-a gentle nudge (or shove as I like to see it) from our greatest self." I also don't really want to be separate or to stick out. In our society, as Orthodox Jews, we stick out, *way out*. My orientation as an Orthodox Jew can be a challenge to me where striving for connection to God can be misunderstood. I often catch people looking at me too, from the corner of their eye. Some have known me since I was young and I'm guessing are baffled by my observance or odd dress code. Or some can't place me as to whether I'm really observant. I don't always fit anywhere. That confuses people and sometimes they feel sorry for me. But, they shouldn't. Perhaps there is something resonating inside them as well? Perhaps we are all reaching for the same connection? Perhaps they are already there and put in my path for me to learn? And, to be honest, I didn't choose this path on my own. I became Orthodox out of sense of obligation... and guilt. I didn't understand how to love God. I thought I should be calling all the shots, not God, not the Torah and definitely not a bunch of rabbis who didn't know me. I'm not suggesting that I now have it all figured out.

Over twenty years ago, I wrote an essay about God and I humbly share it. It went something like this:

God (November 1990)

"I'd like to write about God, but I'm not sure what it is. My thoughts change day to day and sometimes I feel totally disconnected. This world is so physical that it's difficult to understand anything else. Perhaps God is love-that is UNCONDITIONAL love. It's very scary to put God onto paper like this-it's almost like committing yourself to a certain belief. There are always those who have said and say they talk to God. I tend to think they talk with themselves, and if we really listen to our hearts, it is God who is speaking. Yes, I believe God speaks to us through our hearts. It's kind of crazy that we all mumble prayers, which other people wrote. If God is in our hearts than God knows, we're saying someone else's words.

No one else can tell you how to feel about God. But, it's funny how everyone wants you to understand and show you their interpretation of God. I think it's then that God is not around, because you're trying to put someone else's heart inside your own-liking flushing out God. It's scary to think that God is not controlling everything. I mean it would be easy to just say, "Well, God will take care of everything." If God is within us, we must make the conscious choices. I am not sure that God and religion have a lot to do with one another. I believe there have been times when God has touched our lives. I believe the

183

Torah to be God's work, but I often question our interpretations.

I believe the oral law is divine and was meant to remain oral. I believe our intentions to make the physical more spiritual have often turned out to making the spiritual more physical. I believe God is accessible. I believe the Torah to be a gift. Choosing to live by this gift is challenging to say the least. I believe the way some people live today has little to do with God and a lot to do with personal comfort and control. I am not sure how people decide right from wrong without a code of law except that in the absence of religion, perhaps there is a way that exists that we all internally know. Maybe the Torah came because we forgot the way. But these are my beliefs and I just don't know."

Those were my thoughts over twenty years ago. Most, I still hold by. And now, I ask myself, "So what do I believe?" It is funny, the word, "believe." It requires a leap of faith. "Emunah" (faith) is the essence of the English word "Amen." The Hebrew letters of amen (אמן): aleph, mem, nun come from the first and middle letters of the Hebrew alphabet. "Emet" (truth: אמת) covers the entire alphabet (first, middle and last letters). It represents all that there is. It is as if, to believe, we have to have a leap of faith that everything from the middle to the end will be taken care of for us. So, "emunah" (faith, belief) is not exactly a knowing or a hoping, it's a trust.

But, here is what I know: I know that on this planet you have less than a 0.2% chance of being born a Jew. Being Jewish is a gift and an obligation wrapped up in one. Orthodox Judaism is a service, front line army service. It is the God Squad. I cannot tell you exactly what God is, nor would I be so bold as I was twenty years ago to try, but we are His squad. I do know that God expects us to rise above nature and live by his laws. Those laws help us access the Divine. Twenty years ago I didn't think those laws applied to me. I thought rules were "made to be broken." I thought they were a nice history lesson, but not relevant today.

Today, I believe that those laws are a love language from God. Everything that seems natural such as popping food into your mouth, preparing food, certain types of relationships, sleeping in late and so on are redirected by the Torah. We are asked to rise above what may seem natural and doing so brings us to a higher level of consciousness. Much like a miracle is above nature, we as Jews, are asked to go beyond what is natural. This life is not an easy life. It is a service to God. It provides responsibility and boundaries to your citizenship as a human being. It is rich. There is mysticism, depth and truth within the confines of being an Orthodox Jew, that it is hard not to become more spiritual and closer to God if you spend time living this way. We believe that God created the world with sparks of holiness. We spend our days and sometimes nights trying to understand and spread the holiness to the mundane and tapping into the divine while battling our lower inclinations. Although this can be done from just about any religious perspective, it is Jewish observance that creates the "how to" for a Jew to live a spiritual life here on earth. The gematria (numerical value) for halacha and kli (vessel) are the same. It's the halacha (aka mitzvot) that act as vessels for us to return to our source and to show our love to the Almighty.

Sometimes it seems that as Orthodox Jews, we simply thrive off any sort of structure, detail, law and order. The truth is we can get pretty excited about finding a bug on a leaf of lettuce, searching for the perfect etrog or what time we light our candles. But, without spirituality and love, our observance may not deliver the intended message. Without love as its foundation, observance does not work. This is not to discount us for trying, or those whose scrupulous observance can catapult them towards people and towards God. For most of us, though, Orthodoxy is not just a way of living, it is a "soul jacket." There is a place for every Jewish soul and both the mitzvot and the spiritual awareness are necessary to reap the benefits of closeness to the Almighty. According to the Jewish calendar, the Jewish people have a limited time to complete our mission for this world. That is scary. Our 6,000-year calendar is running out.

Yet, so many fall off this path or just run away. It is tough. Just a trip to the grocery store or the holidays alone can have you reaching for a tranquilizer. But, take a moment to listen, ponder, learn and to observe with intention and you will know that there is something holy and authentic. Being close to God or religious comes in so many different forms. There are billions of spiritual paths and even other religions. We can be spiritual, loving, kind, happy, esoteric, and the list goes on. But, living as a Jew, as God's servant, is not left up to our own interpretation. To be holy, there is a code of living, a divine code of law. There is a formula. Orthodox Judaism clearly defines those terms. To be an observant Jew you need to be committed to God and his way of living. You also need to have the support of a strong community and spiritual leaders. In addition, you must understand that the observance is a conduit, a vessel to God and not your ticket to nirvana here on earth.

Within Orthodoxy, I have seen the kind and the not so kind, the truthful and the not so truthful, the good, the bad, the awesome and yes the "chutzpah!" I have played all those parts, as well. There are also many aspects I do not understand or relate to as yet. There are things I just don't like because they are still so foreign to me. In addition, I have tried to keep up with my Super-Man-Hasid-Husband, which has not been easy. In addition, my reception to his needs has not always been so kind. I brought a lot of baggage and insecurities into my marriage that presented a barrier toward anything and anyone that did not feel good. And, as an avoider I have challenged his thinking hoping he'd perhaps give in. Yet we have both grown, and he knows now that I am generally sincere. He is patiently encouraging while I am learning, even if at times, I baffle him with my questions.

My challenge has been in trying to "be" Orthodox. Early on I simply did what I thought was best to survive. My focus was doing what everyone expected of me: stop touching the lights on the Sabbath, cover your head, wear a long skirt, study Torah and pray. I learned at a young age to pacify people, and like many of my qualities, these can be used to benefit or to fault. There are moments that I have felt connected. Yet, there are also times I have felt so very lost. And, as much as I admire it, there are times that standing amongst other religious people, I feel quite undeserving and scared. I then feel as if maybe I'm just acting out a part. As a baal teshuva, I have often felt somewhat like a sling slot wondering when I would be propelled forward. Sometimes the idea of propulsion is frightening. I know this, though. I am not alone. It is not uncommon for someone new to Orthodoxy, to feel "left-out", overwhelmed or as if my spouse is out having an affair with the Torah or "his people." It is also not uncommon to feel exhilarated, connected, spiritual and elevated at the same time. It is not easy and still today I am learning, struggling, reaching, celebrating and contemplating sometimes from my darkest moments. But mostly, I am learning about myself. We all have a struggle whether it is our upbringing, finances, marriage, addictions, sexuality or emotional integrity. Some of those challenges are innate or environmental, and some of them we bring on ourselves. From my own experiences, I have learned not to judge. Our challenges are our best teachers. To grow, we have to wax and wane. We have to experience good and bad, high and low, darkness and light, death and rebirth. We cannot experience the joy without the hard work. And the time is now.

As Mordechai once told me, our Torah is like a letter found in a bottle, a letter from God to the Jewish people. Orthodoxy is a way of life manifested from the Torah, the doctrine of God's will. We all arrive with soul work to do here in this life. Perhaps, we have different talents, gifts and interests, but I believe, we all have a common purpose.

God gave us the Torah with love and to teach us to love: how to love others, how to love the world He gave us, how to love ourselves and how to show our love to God. We do that by honoring the commandments and giving praise. We are the original people of "praise." The root of the word Yehuda (Jew) is Hoda and actually means to give thanks, to praise. It has taken me forty-nine years to understand that all those seemingly strange commandments not only transcend nature, but they are an expression of God's love, protection for our eternal souls; and although mastering 613 of them is an enormous task, we have to try. Yet, the commandments are not God himself. It is not the end. It is a means. Orthodox Judaism is an expression of the Jewish blueprint for creating a tabernacle to the Almighty in ourselves, in our homes and in this world, a conduit to a relationship with God prescribed to us thousands of years ago and interpreted and discussed over and over again until this very day. Orthodox Judaism in its best form expresses itself with love, with commitment, with joy and with praise.

My husband would call that living as a…. Yid.

White Zinfindel

> *I have a bottle of white zinfandel that is sitting on my shelf in our pantry. It is a gift that keeps showing back up in our house every few weeks. I'm sure it's the same bottle. In fact, I think it's been circulating around our community for fifteen years. No one really likes white zinfandel for Kiddush and to be honest no one really likes it with the meals we serve. No one really knows what to do with it except our rabbi who mixes it with a few other horrible tasting wines to stretch the Kiddush wine out to serve the forty plus people sitting at his table. I'm not a wine connoisseur. In fact, the only wine I really like is a sweet bubbly wine. A few years ago a kosher sweet bubbly wine started to become popular and now everyone buys it. It's like drinking over priced lemonade. I actually like it a lot.*

Every once in a while my husband decides we need REAL wine. So he'll order some expensive fancy wine and offer it to people at our Shabbos table. About two people will drink it because everyone really wants the overpriced lemonade. Then it will sit on the top of our refrigerator until my twins run through the kitchen and bang into the refrigerator door sending it crashing onto the floor. Anyway, when people come over our house or we go to someone's house, it is customary to take a small gift or food item. If you get a bottle of white zinfandel, it's usually because the giver grabbed it at the last minute before running out the door. I know because I've done so myself. My husband would like to get rid of the "token gift giving." If everyone stops dropping off tokens no one will feel compelled to do so. He's right, but it just doesn't feel kosher to come empty handed. I've dropped off pickle jars, tomatoes, cookies, etc. I have even dropped off Shabbos toilet paper, a seriously coveted item around orthodox communities.

Now Shabbos toilet paper falls into the "niceties" category and that may include things that smell nice like soap or candles. Recently, I received a little package of little candles. I have no idea what to do with them. They smell nice. I will keep them for when the lights go out. Once, I received a little butter knife. Cute. I don't think it ever made it to our butter. Candy of course is a huge hit with my kids. It's just that I have to monitor it or I'm pulling them off the walls. I used to ask my host, "What can I bring?" That is the nicest thing to do as then you can actually bring what they need. But, often, I will get a reply like, "Well, what do you like to make?" The truth is that I don't like to cook or bake at all. I've been asked three times this past week to make food for families who have just had new babies. I'm practically running a short order kitchen. The other day I offered to make a meal for a family. There are three people living in their house. I inquired, *"How many people will be eating?"* The reply was, *"Ten."* Ten?? Oi vey! So, when I get an invitation, I like to take advantage of the break. I don't ask and I just show up with a gift and hope it's user-friendly or else they have enough sense to pass it along. I'm not alone in this strategy.

I am trying very hard not to pass the white zinfandel back around. I've even Googled what to do with left over wine. Some options were: make salad dressing, make syrup and pour over ice cream or use in beef stew. My favorite was to freeze into little ice cubes and then use it to flavor soups and other dishes. I don't know. I think I'll just let it sit for a while. I'm feeling like I'm going to need to drink it soon enough. My husband is planning another trip to New York.

Afterword

So, here we are…just a few years later.

This is the photo my husband likes to show to some of "his people." He's come a long way allowing our little dog, Cloe in the picture.

My oldest son, Lev, is proud of his tie. It adds color to our family. But, the truth is, we all add *color*…each in our own unique way.

And here's the one I like to show "my people," of course with our dog....She's still recovering from the whole rabbi-dog-swap-episode.

I insisted we take a bright red couch outside. I thought it was time *I* shook things up a bit. The kids revolted. I won.

As I write this, my husband is planning another trip to see the Rebbe, his Rebbe, our Rebbe.

And me?

Well, I'm planning another blog.

Glossary

These definitions just may add some clarity and, of course, a bit of humor too.

Ani L'dodi V'dodi Li: This is the love poem between God and the Jewish people. It's the very original "Roses are red....and violets are blue." Literally, it means "I am my beloved and my beloved is mine," from Song of Songs written by King Solomon.

Ariel: Lion of God. But, it is also the name of our little shul, which is not so little any more in Dunwoody, Georgia.

Ashkenazi: Jews originating from Eastern Europe who, by and large, eat knishes and are much more uptight than their Sephardic counterparts who eat burekas.

Baal Teshuva (BT): A secular, assimilated Jew who is returning to observance of the Torah and the commandments, often like a bulldozer, plowing down any relative or non-observant Jew who stands in their way.

Beis Midrash: This is the battlefield (aka: study hall) where men (or women in some more progressive environments) study the Torah.

Bekeshe: Long, black, silk caftan worn by Hasidic men that looks like they forgot to take off their pajama robe. There are two types: 1) plain black used for davening (praying) 2) Tish bekeshe worn at the dinner table and at the Rebbes tish. It is black with a design and sometimes confused with the smoking jacket of the 1940's.

B'nei Torah: A term used to describe those who are scrupulous in their study of and observance of the Torah. These scholars often sacrifice much in their pursuit of the holy word.

Blech: It sounds like "blah" and clearing your throat mixed together, but it's just a metal sheet used to cover a flame on the Sabbath to remind you that you may warm food, but not cook on the Sabbath.

Bochur: Term used for unmarried men and boys. See b'nei torah.

Burekas: Sephardi pastry filled with a variety of yummy fillings like meat, spinach, rice, potato, cheese or eggplant. Watch out for the "bureka ladies." They'll run you over going for their favorite filling.

Challah: Special braided bread eaten on the Sabbath and holidays. You must have two at each meal. They are often made with three braids having kabbalistic significance, although they can be made with four or six braids as well. It is said that Sarah (yes the biblical one) had piping hot challah in her tent 24/7... sort of like Motel 6 but with fresh bread.

Chatima Tova: Literally means, "a good seal," but is usually translated as, "May you be sealed for a good life in the year to come." This expression is used during Yom Kippur day so that we may be sealed in the book of life.

Chavurah: A loosely structured group (often granola Jews) who get together to pray and celebrate. Usually without rabbinic leadership.

Chesed: Acts of loving kindness and good will between people. Whether you're on the receiving or giving part, there is power in chesed.

Cholent: Traditional meat and barley stew served hot at the Sabbath afternoon meal. Delicious when hot, but often mistaken for brick mortar when allowed to cool. Warning: do not store or try to eat after Shabbos.

Cholov Yisroel: This is a stringency that one takes upon himself to only eat dairy products that have been supervised during production by a Jew

D'vrei Torah: Words of Torah given over to the others sitting at the Shabbos table. For some it's a soap box (like your Uncle Isadore who finally gets a chance to have an attentive audience); but for most, it makes Shabbos or a holiday meal more than a social meal.

Elul: The month before Rosh Hashana that is dedicated to repentance. For orthodox or observing Jews it makes Rosh Hashana come an entire month early.

Erev: The day and evening before a holiday or Shabbos. God created "EVENING and morning." So, we start all holidays in the evening.

Eruv: A boundary around an established Orthodox community.

Etrog: This is no lemon. It's a citron, used on the holiday of Succot.

Frum (FFB): Someone born Orthodox and presumably observant of the commandments from birth. Baal Teshuvas yearn to have the status of an FFB and FFBs claim to stand in the shadows of a Baal Teshuva.

Ganza Mispacha: The whole family, including your great uncle Irving.

Gefen: Vine. Each Jewish holiday or event is sanctified over the "fruit of the vine," (aka wine).

Gemara: Massively large volume of Jewish law and thought that is the primary text taught in Yeshiva. In general, it is taught to boys beginning in the 4th-6th grade.

Gematria: Numerology, where every letter in the Hebrew alphabet is represented by a number. Any Hebrew word will have a corresponding numerical value. Gematria is the original math tutor.

Gezundheit: Literally: health (in German). This is the equivalent of "God Bless You," for when someone sneezes.

Halacha: Jewish law encompassing all facets of the 613 commandments in the Torah. They are like arrows targeting a divine bullseye.

Haimish: Homestyle. Like your grandmothers house.

Hamotzie: Blessing made over bread.

Hasid: Ultra-Orthodox Jew who follows the mystical teachings of the Baal Shem Tov to gain closeness to God. They tend to wear black coats and furry hats, sing and dance a lot. They can put you in your happy place. Go forth and find yourself a Hasid. You won't be sorry.

Havdallah: Prayer marking the end of Shabbos and the return to the regular week.

Hechsher: Little symbol on boxed or packaged items showing that the contents are certified kosher. There are about 500 of them around the world and around 100 in any community.

Jew: Descendant of Abraham, Isaac and Jacob (and for liberal women: of Sarah, Rebecca, Rachel and Leah), required to adhere to 613 biblical and commentated and commentated and commentated commandments.

Jewish: Sort of like a Jew.

Kehila: Congregation. Often used to refer to the synagogue.

Kiddush: The blessing over the wine said on Shabbos or holidays. Pass the Manishevitz, please.

Kiddush Table: food set out after morning prayers on the Sabbath (between first and second meals) because we haven't had enough to eat (and to remember it's the Sabbath, as if our stomachs could forget).

Kiftayas: Sephardic meatballs.

Kiddush Hashem: A toast to the Almighty. Well, really it's just living like a mensch!

Kippah: Yarmulka in Yiddish. Skullcap worn by Jewish males. Comes in a variety of forms from covering the entire head in a rainbow of colors, to knit, to satin (from cousin Jake's bar mitzvah), to felt (often all black or black decorated for little kids).

Kiruv: Outreach. The act of bringing non-orthodox Jews back to the Torah. Just offer food and they will come.

Kishke: You don't want to know.

Kli: Vessel.

Kol Nedrei: Very solemn service during the evening of Yom Kippur (day of Atonement) where we are absolved of any vows we may have made during the past year.

Kosher: Fit, allowed. Adheres to the biblical law of what may be eaten. It would take an entire book to explain. It's a lot more than pickles and bagels, but, basically, we don't eat milk with meat (no goat cooked in its mother's milk), no piggies, no shellfish, no swarmy or crawly things like beetles. There are about three commandments turned into three hundred.

Kugel: Jewish casserole. Potato or noodle. Each square of kugel adds about five pounds to your waist.

Lain: Yiddish for "read." To read from the Torah during services.

Lubuvatcher: Sect of Chassidim that originated in the city of Lubuvatch in Russia. Now headquartered in Crown Heights, Brooklyn. They have outreach centers all over the world.

Maoz Tzur: Rock of Ages. Song sung after lighting the Chanukah candles.

Mashiach: Messiah, may he arrive speedily in our days. We're waiting.....

Matzah: Unleavened bread eaten on Pesach. Taste like cardboard. Good cardboard, but cardboard.

Matzah Ball: Like a dumpling made from matzah meal (ground matzah). They come in light and fluffy and cannonball. Your stomach can tell the difference.

Melacha: Creative activity forbidden on the Sabbath. There are thirty-nine categories. For example, we don't turn on and off light switches, which falls under the category of "building," as in building a circuit. Learn these thirty-nine forbidden tasks, integrate them into your Sabbath and you are home free.

Melamed: Teacher or tutor.

Melava Malka: Meal eaten by Chassidim after the Shabbos is over, because they can't get "enough of that lovin' feeling," (toward God).

Mensch: Be a man! (or a woman). Just, be nice.

Mezuzot: Scroll containing two paragraphs from the Torah that is biblically commanded to be placed on most doors in your house, sans the bathroom.

Michitza: Partition separating the men and women during services. It creates a spiritual separation for men and women but can send a non-religious person running out the back door. You may find singles peeking across the michitza.

Midrash: Compilation of commentaries and stories that are used to teach a lesson.

Mikvah: Ritual bath used to remove impurities and purify the soul. No massage. No bubbles. Just the bath.

Mishkan: Tabernacle erected in the desert and used until the first Temple was built in Jerusalem. This edifice was schlepped wherever the Jewish people went.

Mishloach Manot: Package containing at least two ready to eat foods distributed on Purim day to promote harmony and brotherly love. Of course two becomes twenty-two and oi vey! We forgot Cousin Edith!

Mitzvot: Commandments. There are 613 biblical and seven rabbinic. They are like shooting arrows to the Almighty with love.

Naaseh V'nishma: Literally: We will do and we will hear. Phrase in the Torah showing the Jews readiness to accept the Torah before they knew all of what was contained therein. Sort of like when you sign a marriage document before YOU know what you're doing.

Niggun: Tune with no words sung by Hasidim as a way to connect to God. It may bolt you awake or lull you to sleep.

Oneg: Delight. Usually referring to the delight of Sabbath and holidays.

Or Ve Shalom: Light and Peace. A very awesome Sephardic synagogue located in Atlanta, Ga.

Parsha: The Torah is divided into weekly portions. Each one is called the Parsha of the Week.

Pareve: Not containing meat or milk, so you can eat a pareve food with either meat or milk.

Pas Yisroel: A stringency placed upon oneself to only eat grain products that were baked under Jewish supervision.

Payos: Sidelocks of hair from each side of the head that is biblically forbidden to shave (Lev chap 19). Hasidim grow them long. Really cool people grow them super long. Makes Jews look a bit like sheep. The Lord *is* our Shepherd.

Pesach: The Hebrew version of the holiday known as Passover.

Rabbi: Spiritual leader and advisor at a congregation or synagogue. Sometimes like a teacher. Sometimes like a father. Sometimes like Jiminy Cricket....your conscious.

Rebbe: Spiritual leader of a sect of Hasidim.

Rebbeim: Plural of Rebbi or Rabbi

Rebbetzin: Behind every great rabbi is an amazing wife. Rabbi's or Rebbe's wife.

Rosh Chodesh: First of the month commemorated with extra praises. Often known as a holiday for women as a reward to our not having participated in the golden calf fiasco.

Schach: Natural limbs or leaves used to cover a sukkah.

Schlep: Yiddish for "drag," or "carry."

Sephardic: Jews originating from Spain, the Middle East and North Africa who eat burekas and are much more laid back than Ashkenazi Jews who eat knishes. The best looking Jews by far.

Seudah: Festive meal with about eight courses, schnapps, divrei torah.

Seudat Hamafseket: The meal eaten before the fast on Tisha B'av.

Shabbaton: A Shabbos getaway with friends or particular group of people.

Shabbos: The seventh day of the week. The day of rest. No, not that kind of rest. Also called Shabbat or Sabbath.

Shadchan: Matchmaker, and she expects a large fee.

Sheitel: Wig worn by religious or observant women. No sheitel. No eat at your house.

Shiva: Seven days of mourning after the passing of a parent, spouse, sibling or child.

Shnoring: The act of begging or seeking a hand out.

Shnorrer : One who engages in schnorring.

Shteibel: A little room or little house used for prayer or Torah study.

Shul: Synagogue.

Simcha: Joyous occasion like a wedding, bar mitzvah, bat mitzvah or bris.

Simchas Beis Hashoeva: The water celebration during the holiday of sukkos. Sort of like a water party. The Talmud says, "Someone who has never seen the joy of a Simchas Beis Hashoeva, has never seen joy in their life."

Simchat Torah: Jewish holiday that celebrates the Torah with dancing and concludes the high holidays.

Snood: Pre-tied scarf or more like a rag. It's like wearing a big sign that says, "I'm trying really hard to be observant but didn't feel like dressing up today, so I put this rag on my head. Get over it."

Streimel: Big bird's nest on top of those "men in black." Ok, really it's a large fur hat worn by married men on the Sabbath and holidays.

Sofer: Jewish scribe. Serious religious artist. No mistakes made. Details and design matter.

Sukkah: Temporary dwelling with an organic roof that represents the clouds of glory.

Tefillin: Phylacteries (who made that word up?). Boxes containing specially written parchments that are worn by men during weekday morning prayers.

Tichel: An upgrade of a snood.

Tish: Literally: Table. Refers to Hasidim gathering around their rebbe on the Sabbath and holidays. They eat, sing, praise and if lucky, get a bracha (blessing) from the rebbe.

Tovel: To immerse dishes in a mikva as commanded in the book of Numbers.

Traif: Not kosher. WARNING: DO NOT EAT IT! Whew....that was close.

Tzedakah: Charity

Tzizit: Special fringed garment worn by males as commanded in Numbers. It is the original, God ordained, finger fidget.

Vidui: Confessing. As soon as you're done, just start all over.

Yiddishkite: General term for authentic Torah Judaism

Acknowledgements

So, this is the part of the book that most people don't read, but the truth is there are so many people who helped me along the way. The hard part with writing the acknowledgments is figuring out when you actually started writing the book and not leaving anyone out. Truthfully, I would have to go back to my birth or at least the beginning of time to really give proper thank yous and that would really take way too long. So, I'll just start with when I actually wrote this book, which at this point seems like a long time ago. There is of course, my husband, who provided me with the subject to write this book. I must not only thank him for his personality, support, love and drive but also his amazing (and often annoying) attention to detail.

I had several other editors along the way. I'd like to thank my holy brother-in-law, Mike Rechtman for his insights, editing skills and support as well as encouraging me to actually write this book myself. I'd also like to thank Karen Adler and Sylvia Miller for editing my early editions.

I'd like to thank Rabbi Binyomin and Dena Friedman for not only reading through my manuscript and being a moral compass in a not so moral world, but for never giving up on their mission. I'd like to thank all the wonderful people at Ariel. I sometimes cannot believe I landed in such an amazing community.

I could not pass up thanking all the wonderful teachers and mentors in my life. I cannot list them all but I'd like to draw particular attention to the following teachers who have both moved and inspired me to reach within: Rabbi Binyomin Friedman, Rebbetzin Dena Friedman, Rabbi Michoel Friedman, Rebbetzin Miriam Feldman, Rebbetzin Rivka Freitag, Rebbetzin

Lori Palatnik, Rabbi Lazer Brody, Reb Shomo Carlebach, Rabbi Doniel Katz and Rabbi David Fohrman and Chana Rudnick.

Thank you to my friends who supported me along this journey: you know who you are! If I start listing you, I will for sure leave someone out and have to go beat my chest and write apologies. So, yes, this is for you. Thank you!!

I'd like to thank, Debra Sifen, for her amazing artistic abilities and friendship. No one can quite make me chuckle from a drawing like she can. Oh, and Debra, don't worry...I'm working on my "doggening."

I'd like to thank Carmelle Danneman for the front cover photo.

I'd like to thank our siblings: Morris, Sheryl, Alisa and Stuart (and their spouses: Amy, Mike, Scott and Lu) for lending an ear, encouraging me to write and being supportive through every phase of my life (including reading my poems when I was younger). Thank you to Aunt Joan, Alicia and Joe. You taught me so much about "family."

Thank you to all of our children for giving me plenty to write about, their humor, their support and being the best kids ever!!! Thank you for being so patient to let me write: Lev, Carmelle, Rafi and Nissim: you rock my world!

Cloe...my sweet little dachshund...thank you for your love and warmth and for staying up with me so many late nights (well, under the covers) while I wrote.

Thank you Mom and Aba for bringing me into this amazing world filled with so many experiences, and for giving me the wings to learn and experience on my own.

You planted me –A Tree
Colors So Clear
Branches That Reach
To Dance with the Wind
Roots to Drink
From Knowledge Within
Life Which Bore Life
Your Gift: mine
To Nurture-Your Task
Mine-To Ask
Differences Learned
Respect to be earned
Seasons Provide
A Tree Fully Grown
Not Appearance Alone

Most importantly thank God, the Almighty, the source of all. What a wild and crazy journey this is. Thank you for not giving up on me. I cherish every moment here.

The Puppeteer

We are often not aware of the Puppeteer who steadies our every thought. I think we are like puppets and God is the puppeteer. We can move our own parts and control our own thoughts but the Puppeteer is always there if we need a thought. Some of us never give thought to our Puppeteer. Some of us do but never pull on our puppet strings and some of us pull every moment we can and I think that makes the Puppeteer very happy.

Book Club Discussion

If you're part of a book club and are one of the people who actually read books, these questions might just strike up a great conversation. If you're one of those who come for the cookies and tea, well, maybe starting with the questions is not such a bad idea anyway.

Do we all have a common purpose here?

What *is* the mission of the Jewish people?

How does it differ from that of other religions?

Why did we receive the Torah?

What are we to do with the Torah?

What is the connection between Love and Commitment?

What if your spouse or someone you are committed to has a journey that is very different than yours?

Why is our divorce rate so high? What is the impact?

What sort of things, purpose or missions are you committed to?

About the Author (and her yid)

When not blogging (marrietoayid.com), schlepping, carpooling, cooking for Shabbos (she does not follow recipes), or working, Ilana is trying to keep THE YID in line. Her latest task is monitoring the number of rebbe photos that keep showing up in her house. Ilana loves spending time with family, friends and the Ariel community. She also enjoys hiking (not too far), biking (not too far), walking her dog (not to far), tap dancing and creating solutions for kids with special needs (she currently works as a creative director/writer/physical therapist). She can be reached at kitov18@gmail.com. This is her first book.

Mordechai (aka: THE YID), can be reached at sofer36@gmail.com, the torahdepot.com. You may find him writing mezuzahs, tefillin and Torah; laining (chanting) or studying Torah, talking to total strangers about yiddishkite, or wandering around a Hasidic shteibel (town) somewhere looking for more of his people.

About the Illustrator:

Proud to have known Ilana and Mordechai since third grade, Debra Sifen admits that while they were spelling, she was probably doodling. Amidst a scattered journey of illustrating and cartooning, mothering, cooking, homeschooling and doing dishes, Debra has published & illustrated several children's books including *Who Wants Life?* , *Manny's a Thief*, and *Then I Got 3 Scoops*. She currently makes her home in Toronto with her husband, still feeding her 3 children and her dog, Sammy. You can enjoy more of her cartoons at www.seaweedsoasis.com and *Hair of the Dog Comics* on Facebook.

Made in the USA
Charleston, SC
06 July 2014